Easy Soap Making

Create 100% Pure and Beautiful Soaps with The Nerdy Farm Wife's Easy Recipes and Techniques

Carmela Scott

The information stated herein is provided for educational purposes exclusively. The presentation of the data is without contractual agreement or any kind of warranty assurance.

All trademarks inside this book are for clarifying purposes only and are possessed by the owners themselves, not allied with this document.

Disclaimer

All erudition supplied in this book is specified for educational and academic purposes only. The author is not in any way to be responsible for any outcomes that emerge from using this book. Constructive efforts have been made to render information that is both precise and effective, but the author is not to be held answerable for the accuracy or use/misuse of this information.

Foreword

I will like to thank you for taking the very first step of trusting me and deciding to purchase/read this life-transforming book. Thanks for investing your time and resources on this product.

I can assure you of precise outcomes if you will diligently follow the specific blueprint I lay bare in the information handbook you are currently checking out. It has transformed lives, and I firmly believe it will equally change your own life too.

All the information I provided in this Do It Yourself piece is easy to absorb and practice.

INTRODUCTION

Something is satisfying about making a batch of natural soap. Not only do you feel the complete satisfaction of creating something charming yourself, but you also understand precisely what active ingredients your soap includes because you put everything together.

When you visit the grocery store to get a few of the items to be used throughout the day, do you take so much time observing the ingredients? Do you check out the prices and feel like it is a big dupe and that you aren't getting the value that you really should out of these items? More people are getting tired of the prices, harmful chemicals, and absence of choices that they are getting at the store with some of their health and beauty products, and they are choosing to make some of these on their own at their homes.

Do you want to make soap and just do not know where to start? Most people had to browse the Internet for a long time before getting up the nerve to make their first batch of soap. But as they produced more quantities, they had increasingly more concerns no one appeared to have the answers to. Whenever someone raved and attempted a new oil, they bought that same oil, until they had a store filled with many different oils! Such people usually have a lot of questions-- why use a specific oil? What makes one oil any much better than another one?

The interest in natural homemade beauty help has blown up over the last few years. More and more people are discovering every day that there is another option to consumer-oriented beauty items that you purchase in the store, a lot of which have chemicals with unpronounceable names and doubtful efficacy. Having the ability to show you this option is the most significant reason for this book.

With this book, you will learn a great deal about making your natural bath bombs. And this will leave you much better geared up to look after the health needs of both you and your household quickly. With just a little effort and the best information, you will be amazed at what you can achieve.

This book will look at how you can make some of your bath bombs in your home. Bath bombs are types of soap that you have the ability to add essential oils to and other active ingredients that will change the way you bathe. These small bombs just need to be dropped into the bathwater, and once the fizzing is all done, you will be able to delight in a healthy bath that makes your skin feel incredible and can assist with relaxation, skin problems, depression, energy, and a lot more.

This book will explore all the things that you need to know when it concerns working with these bath bombs. Understanding what these bath bombs are, how to make them, a few of the typical issues that develop these bath bombs as a novice, benefits of using bath bombs and how they can improve your life, and even some of the advantages of making these at home are simply a few of the topics that we will go over inside this guidebook. Besides, we will have a look at some of the best bath bomb recipes that you can develop at home to help you feel incredible and to see how easy it is to make these bath bombs.

When you are ready to start learning all that you can about and wish to start making a few of your own from home, take a look through this guidebook and see how simple the process can be and even find out some terrific recipes that are going to make it a lot easier than before!

All the best, as you learn what it takes to make your first batch of bath bombs.

CHAPTER ONE

Introduction To Soap Making

How Soap Is Made

Soap is made when the reaction of lye together with water also reacts with oil and turns the fat into salt. This process is referred to as saponification, and It can take about 24 to 48 hours for the cold process soap to saponify. For the hot process, the saponification becomes complete when it's finished cooking. A bar soap can not be made without alkalis, salt hydroxide and liquid soap can not be made without potassium hydroxide. If used poorly, both are caustic and can be dangerous.

The caustic part isn't something to be afraid of, but it has to be appreciated. All safety equipment and all security treatments must be made use of throughout the entire soap-making process. Carelessness to take correct security precautions can trigger injuries. It is advisable to wait till the kids are at school, your spouse is at work, and the pets are outdoors or closed in another part of your home before you begin making soap.

When our grandmas made soap, it was just a guesstimate in how much lye was to be used. Now, there are soap calculators that calculate how much lye is required. This implies no more guessing and saying goodbye to worries. With the appropriate usage of a soap calculator, you'll feel that your soap will not be lye-heavy. With SoapCalc, for example, you discover how to create a bar of soap to be precisely what you want.

Fundamental Soap Ingredients

The appeal of soap is that you need extremely few components for a simple bar of soap. Fragrance, color, and ingrained pieces are great add-ins, but here's all you need to make a bar of soap:

These are the bases of your soap.

Castor oil: is used for adding lather and moisturizing. Several other oils/butter can be used for adding more conditioning to the soap.

Lye: This consists of salt hydroxide for bar soap and potassium hydroxide for liquid soap. Soap can not be made without it.

Distilled water: This eliminates any contaminants or high quantities of minerals your water might contain.

Borax: This is mainly used to neutralize any remaining lye in liquid soap, improve its cleansing power, and reduce the pH. It is natural in form and mined directly from the earth. Borax is likewise understood to be a disinfectant and deodorizer. Frequently borax is contributed to the hot process or cold process soap when making a mechanic's soap bar.

Adding Some FunTo The Process: Additives

You can get imaginative and add to that standard bar of soap with ingredients like herbs, honey, milk, colors, fragrance, salt, sugar, and micas. Anything aside from oil, lye, and water are useful ingredients.

When dealing with fragrance oils, be sure to make use of only skin-safe fragrance oils. Essential oils can be used in adding fragrance to soap, but make sure it is used sparingly due because they're mighty and can burn the skin if you use excessively.

Be sure to read the section written on essential oils before using them in soap. Any color made use of soap has to be skin safe, and don't use crayons. The majority of oxides remain the same throughout the soap- making process.

The Use of Vinegar

You may be thinking, Vinegar in soap? Not exactly. Although vinegar is not included in the soap, it is crucial to have on hand since vinegar reduces the effects of lye.

Flush entirely with water and follow with vinegar to neutralize and eliminate all traces of the lye if you spill lye on your skin.

If you just flush with water, your skin will have a slick feel. When you use the vinegar properly, the sleek feeling will eventually go away.

The Significance of Safety Equipment

With regards to safety, it's the number-one concern when making soap, and with just a couple of essential economic tools, you can secure yourself from harm.

Shatterproof glass or a face shield. Any type of heat-resistant, wrap-around security goggles will do great. Stay away from the kind of goggles that look similar to spectacles as they tend to warm up and fog over, making it difficult to see what you are doing. A full-face guard also works great and isn't all that pricey. If you put on glasses, the shields are your best option because you can wear them right over your lenses.

Latex gloves like the ones dental professionals or doctors use are mostly the best.

Long-sleeved type of shirt. The splatter from the potassium hydroxide mix or lye can be annoying to the skin, and it can likewise eat holes in clothing, so use an old long-sleeved t-shirt to cover your arms and protect the front of your t-shirt from splatters. You may also wear an apron to safeguard your pants.

Avoid making soap in your bare feet or sandals. Any splatter will scorch your skin and cause serious injuries

Other Soap-Making Equipment You'll Need

Here once again, just a couple of inexpensive items are needed to make soap:

Most of us have pots at the moment and will not have to purchase any. A 3-12-quart cup will enable you to make any size batch of soap you desire.

- **Portable immersion mixer.** An immersion mixer is a compact, sticklike mixer that has one spinning blade at the end. Mainly used for light whipping cream or drinks, they're also a soap maker's best buddy because they lower the amount of stirring time (and save your arm!). However, they're optional if you would rather Stir-It-Yourself (SIY).

- **Whisk or Spoon:** Stainless steel is best, or you can make use of utensils made for nonstick pans. Over time, the wood becomes dry, and little fragments will end up in the soap batch.

- **Spatula:** Nonstick or stainless is finest.

- **Bowls**: Plastic or stainless-steel bowls are the best to use to measure oils, butter, water, or lye. The added lids that reduce the opportunity of spills if the container gets turned over or bumped. Some people use a high plastic pitcher with a cover that protects the handle so the pitcher can not be tipped or overturned.

- **Plastic pitcher with a lid**: This is used to mix lye. Don't use a glass pitcher because it will engrave the glass. Lye heats up a lot and could cause the glass to break hazardous situations.

- **Scale:** Everything has to be weighed in the soap-making process. You'll need an excellent electronic kitchen scale with a flat platform, big enough to rest bowls and pitchers on which measures to 1/10 an ounce. It needs to also measure in grams.

- **Stainless-steel thermometer**: A thermometer informs you about the temperature of the oils and the lye/water, so you know when to mix the oils and lye/water. The hotter the oils, the much faster the soap will set up. You can feel the outside if you don't have a thermometer of the pitcher or pot with your fingers. It'll be comfortable to the touch when it's ready to have the lye mix included.

- **Molds**

The Shelf Life of Soap

The iodine level profoundly influences the life span of soap. If the iodine gets too high, it will produce DOS-- DreadOrangeSpots-- a sure sign the cleanser is going rancid.

For soap with a long rack life, pay close attention to the iodine value when you put your soap recipe SoapCalc. The iodine value belongs to the soap qualities.

STORING YOUR SOAP.

The main point to consider when storing soap is that it will absorb scents quickly, so be cautious where you store it. We like to keep our soaps in lidded plastic containers, like plastic shoe boxes. With the cover on, the soap stays tidy, and the fragrance remains real and does not soak up any other scents.

These boxes also stack well in a little space. Be sure to identify packages, consisting of the name of the soap, fragrance, date, and the recipe if you like. It's so simple to forget what's in all those boxes!

If you are a smoker, don't allow the smoke to get near your soap. There's absolutely nothing as wrong as soap that smells like a dirty ashtray!

CHAPTER TWO

Using Fragrance And Essential Oils In Soap Making

Nearly every soap-maker ends up being addicted to and thrilled about fragrances and scent blends. We joke with each other about our enthusiasm that the family doesn't need groceries today because there's a fragrance oil prebuy beginning, and that's more vital than food.

Having Fun With Fragrance Oils

Your children and their friends had messed up the kitchen by the time you returned from work. And you've had a headache all day. You wish to escape from that in a bath filled with the scents of lavender and vanilla in a soap you made yourself. That's where fragrance oils come in.

Fragrance oils are quite relaxing. You may lie in your tub, surrounded by scents, and simply let the world go by. Light a scented candle while you are doing it, and relax much more.

Choose The Right Scent For You

Fragrance oils are artificial blends made from chemicals that imitate scents and essential oils that are then included to bases. Fragrance oils are created in different ways for particular products-- candle lights, bath and body items, and soap.

Below are some of the most common fragrances:

- **Spellbound Woods** is a sexy blend of leading notes of amber, middle notes of cedar and sandalwood, and faint bottom notes hinting a touch of floral.
- **Black Tea and Berries** is a deliciously fruity and fresh blend of berries with an additional red clover touch.
- **Serene Mountain Lake** is a crisp, fresh, and clean water fragrance.
- **Lavender Rose** is a charming blend of French lavender with rose leading notes complimented by moss, budget, and musk. Include a little powdery note, and you have a very romantic, soft, and sexy fragrance.
- **Cucumber Mint** is a rejuvenating mix of fresh mint and crisp, cold, cucumbers.
- **Fresh Pomegranate** is a sweet fruity-cranberry scent.

That's simply a sampling of the more than 7,500 types of fragrances in the market today. Several of them are duplicates of famous perfumes and industrial home fragrance lines. No matter what kind of scent you like, you will certainly discover plenty to pick from.

Safety First

It's essential that you just use fragrances considered to be safe for the skin in your soaps. Ensure you choose your vendor carefully, and know what you're purchasing.

A lot has been said about phthalates in fragrance oils and how damaging these are. There are several types of phthalates, and some are more hazardous than others. They are usually found in some of the bases makers use, but you can find numerous fragrances that are phthalate-free.

Fragrance oils have what are referred to as flashpoints. When an open flame is used, a flashpoint is the temperature level at which the fragrance oil offers off only enough vapor that will spark.

Just how much Do I Use in Soap?

You desire your soap to smell great. However, you don't want it so strong that you get a headache from the scent, so it's essential to understand how much fragrance oil to make use of. As a general guideline, for more powerful fragrance oils, make use of just.5 to.7 ounce per pound of fat.

You will save cash buying the higher-priced oil because you use less fragrance oil per pound of soap. With the cheaper and weaker fragrances, you have to use 1 ounce or more per pound of soap, and even then, the scent may fade within a month or two.

Mixing Fragrance Oils

You can combine or mix fragrances, even those coming from different producers, or include an essential oil to a fragrance oil to make a new fragrance. To make a man's perfume fragrance oil into one appropriate for a female fragrance, all you have to do is add a little floral fragrance oil.

Some soap-makers also add the fragrance oil to the warm oils before adding the lye mixture. Some wait till light trace.

Enhancing the Quality of Soaps with Essential Oils

You might be wondering why essential oil is included in a book on making soap. Essential oils were our very first "medicine," so why not add them to soap to aid with different skin or hair issues? Not just can you use them for medicinal reasons, some of them are also terrific for adding fragrance to the soap.

Do not attempt to use essential oils as if they were fragrance oils. With a growing number of antibiotic-resistant germs, mutating viruses, disease-causing parasites, and infectious fungi in the news, every day, it can be soothing to understand we have essential oils to rely on because, although the mutating bacteria in infections can become resistant to Western medications, they never end up being resistant to essential oils. A study in France revealed the antiseptic qualities of 34 essential oils. Amongst them, thyme, origanum, sweet orange, lemongrass, Chinese cinnamon, and rose were so antibacterial that an individual part of these rendered 1,000 parts of raw sewage without all living organisms.

Though this particular knowledge has been known and applied with fantastic success for ages, it's just now being uncovered. A curious physician put some of the microbe-laden air from a healthcare facility into a flask consisting of a few drops of essential oils, and after 20 minutes, 40 percent of the microorganisms were ruined; 80 percent in an hour, and one hundred percent in 9 hours!

Essential oils need to be called germ-killing oils! They're so good to contribute to soaps for acne and other conditions where bacteria are a problem.

Adding Essential Oils to Soap

Peppermint, clove, and cinnamon all smell good but can have so much negative effect if used excessively. If you wish to have the smell of clove and cinnamon in your soap, then use the cooking herbs you have in the spice rack in the kitchen area instead of essential oils. Or you can purchase a skin-safe fragrance oil that's been formulated for use in soap-making.

When trying to add essential oils to soap, avoid using them as if they were fragrance oils. They are too powerful and might cause a skin issue. Most essential oils should just be made use of at 5 percent and never more than 7 percent.

If you are using essential oils in creams or lotions, it is advisable to buy a book that tells the portions that have been evaluated for every essential oil.

Conventional Essential Oils You Can Use.

Below are a few of the essential oils you can use in your soaps:

Note: This detail isn't indicated to take the vital place of professional medical help. It's just a standard of recognized usages for essential oils.

Balsam Peru (Myroxylonpereirae)- Known uses: Assists in holding fragrance in products; helpful for chapped hands and feet; and eliminates itching triggered by scabies, eczema, and ringworm. Use a percentage at a time.

Basil, sweet (Ocimumbasilicum) antispasmodic, Antibacterial and anti-inflammatory - Known usages: for discomfort relief, chest and virus infections, mouth ulcers, muscle pains, and contaminated gums; functions as a digestion aid; assists rheumatoid arthritis; and aids in circulation and urinary system infections.

Bay laurel (Laurus nobilis) Antiseptic and expectorant - Known usages: for colds, virus infections, muscle aches and pains, sprains, bruises, hair loss, greasy hair, and flaky scalp; can act as a scalp and hair tonic, breathing system inhalant, and liver and kidney tonic. Try it in hair shampoo bars!

Bay rum (Pimento racemosa)- Known uses: for general pains and discomforts, scalp conditions, acne, dandruff, and oily hair; functions as a hunger stimulant; and settles stomach discomforts. Try using it in a hair shampoo bar or gel.

Benzoin (Styrax benzoin) Antiseptic and expectorant - Known uses: as a pulmonary antiseptic; for psoriasis, acne, and eczema; serves as a preservative in foods, and helps hold the fragrance in soap.

Bergamot (Citrus bergamia) Antiseptic, expectorant: Known usages: Relaxes the nervous system; serves as a digestive aid and a gargle for aching throats; helps anxiety, depression, moderate breathing and urinary system infections, herps, wounds, acne, and oily skin.

Cajeput (Melaleuca leucadendron) Antiseptic, analgesic, and expectorant - Known uses: functions as an insect repellant; aids with skincare, wound cleansing; acts as a stimulant; soothes colic and vomiting; and helps respiratory tract infections, nasal and sinus congestion, headaches, gout, muscle tightness, pain, fire ant bites, menstrual cramps, acne, herpes, hemorrhoids, and varicose veins. From the very same household as tea tree and manuka.

Carrot seed (Daucus carota) Stimulant - Known Uses: Functions as a tonic for liver regeneration and cholesterol control; helps fully grown wrinkled skin; tones the skin, stimulates blood cells; adds flexibility to the surface; assists burns, weeping sores, ulcers, boils, eczema, psoriasis, carbuncles, and scars; and can be used as a massage oil and blood cleanser.

Cedarwood, atlas (Cedrusatlantica) Antibacterial.- Known usages: serves as an insecticide; assists to get rid of body fat, cellulite, fluid retention, breathing disorder discomfort, dandruff, oily skin and scalp, alopecia, acne, eczema, kidney and bladder functions, and psoriasis; decreases oily secretions; serves as a hair tonic for seborrhea of the scalp; can be used in chest rubs; assists in holding scents. It can likewise be used in men's fragrances, in tonics, in facial washes and shampoos, and chest rubs. This is a real cedar, also as Atlantic cedar or Moroccan cedarwood.

Cinnamon bark (Cinnamomumzeylanicum) Antibacterial, antispasmodic, antibacterial, aphrodisiac, and antifungal: Known uses: serves as an insecticide and room spray; can be inhaled for a circulatory and breathing stimulant; helps depression and fatigue. The bark oil is considered a dermal toxin, so do not use it on the skin. If you desire a cinnamon- smelling soap, utilize the cinnamon you prepare with instead.

Clary sage (Salvia sclera) Analgesic and antispasmodic: Known uses: helps anxious tension, fear, paranoia, anxiety; relaxes; prevents prolactin; helps throughout menopause; relaxes digestion; accelerates labor; assists throat and breathing infections; cools swelling; and helps hold fragrances in perfumes, soaps, and cosmetics. Do not use while pregnant or nursing.

Combavapetitgrain (Citrus hystrix) Antiseptic and anti-inflammatory. The Known uses: Acts as a liver decongestant and sedative; calms; and eases stress, agitation, insomnia, skin swelling, and acne. You can utilize it in soap for acne.

Coriander (Coriandrum sativum) Anti-inflammatory. Known uses: for tension, anxiety, insomnia, to stimulate the mind, arthritis pain, migraines, clears blackheads, and tames oily skin.

Cypress (Cupressus sempervirens) Antispasmodic and antibacterial. Known uses: acts as a diuretic, deodorant, hemostatic, cryptic, hepatic, vasoconstrictor, sedative, and breathing tonic; can be inhaled for strength and convenience, or diluted in a provider oil and utilized to massage varicose veins every day. Attempt it in an antiperspirant soap!

Elemi (Canarium luzonicum) Antiseptic, Antifungal, analgesic, and expectorant. It's nontoxic, nonirritating, and non-sensitizing. Knownusages: helps nervous exhaustion and stress, skin and acne, cell regrowth, mature and dry skin, wounds, sores, irritated skin, eczema, and dermatitis; balances sebum secretions; and controls heavy perspiration.

Eucalyptus (Eucalyptus globulus) Also called blue gum. Antibacterial, antirheumatic, expectorant, analgesic, and insecticide. Known usages: functions as a decongestant, hinders cold viruses, pushes back pests, lowers fevers, eases breathing, clears sinus blockage, loosens up phlegm, and can be used in room sprays. Must never be taken internally.

Eucalyptus (Eucalyptus radiate) Antiviral and expectorant. Known uses: Same as euca- lyptusbeads. This one is gentler and more enjoyable oil to utilize. For a blend of fragrance, try mixing it with a spearmint.

Eucalyptus, Lemon (Eucalyptus citriodora) antibacterial, antiviral, antifungal, and analgesic. Known uses: assists viral, bacterial, and fungal skin infections; colds and influenza; is soothing; serves as a sedative and an antihypertensive. Useful in soap.

Fir needle (Abies alba) Analgesic, antibacterial, expectorant, antiperspirant. Known usages: breathed in for stress and anxiety, stress, and respiratory problems; is warming; great for massages; and relieves muscle pains, pain, and arthritic or rheumatic conditions.

Fir needle, Canada (Abies Canadensis) - Canadian balsam and Siberian fir are favored for their beautiful fragrance. Known usages: helpful for breathing issues, warming, massages, and antiperspirant and room sprays.

Frankincense (Boswellia carteri) Also known as olibanum. Antiseptic and astringent. Known uses: for anxiety and stress, mature and dry skin, injuries, scars, and wrinkles; functions as a diuretic; assists digestion; and can be used as a sedative.

Geranium (Pelargonium graveolens) a.k.a. Antidepressant, rose geranium, antiseptic, and analgesic. Known uses: helps PMs, anxiety, and stress and anxiety; acts as a diuretic, detoxifier; assists promote the lymphatic system; balances sebum; assists oily skin, ulcers, wounds, and burns; and repels mosquitoes.

Grapefruit, pink (Citrus paradise) Stimulant, antidepressant, antibacterial, disinfectant. Known uses: Helps with depression; functions as a detoxifier and diuretic; helps cellulite, digestion, blockage, oily skin, and acne; and can be used as a room spray.

Jasmine (Jasminum grandiflorum) Antidepressant, aphrodisiac, antibacterial, and antispasmodic. Known usages: Helps to deal with anxiety, headaches, tension, skin dermatitis, eczema, and fear exhaustion.

Juniper berry (Juniperus Communis)antispasmodic, antiseptic, astringent, and expectorant. TheKnown uses: Acts as a diuretic; helps the urinary system, cystitis, kidney stones, gout, acne, obstructed pores, weeping eczema, psoriasis, and inflammations; and eliminates uric acid. The extracts and berries are used in diuretics, laxatives, gout reward- ment, wart treatments, flea and tick repellants, hot scents, and aftershaves.

Lavender (Lavandula officinalis) Known usages: helps burns, headaches, sleep, professional athlete's foot, and herpes and functions as a form of insect repellant.

Lavender, Bulgarian (lavender augustifolia) analgesic, antidepressant, antirheumatic, antiseptic, antispasmodic, antiviral, antibacterial, antifungal, and decongestant. Known uses: serves as a diuretic, deodorant, bactericide, sedative, and fungicide; calms; decreases hypertension; helps insomnia, sunburns, and scars; promotes new skin cells; and can be used in space sprays. It's likewise great in soap!

Lavender, super (Lavandula hybrid var. extremely French) Antispasmatic. Known uses: It helps to deal with headaches, inflammation, relaxation, acne, scabies, skin infections, and respiratory disorders. It's excellent in soap!

Lavendin, Grosso (Lavandula hybrid var. Grosso French) Antiseptic and anti-inflammatory. Known uses: serves as a stimulant; helps acne, scabies, skin infections, and breathing disorders. This is fantastic in soap.

Lemongrass (Cymbopogon citrates) Anti-inflammatory. TheKnown uses: Helps high blood pressure, gastrointestinal problems, and fever; it can be utilized in antiperspirants, skincare, fragrances, and insect repellants; also excellent for aromatherapy.

Lemongrass, East Indian (Cymbopogon flexuous) Anti-inflammatory. This genus has200 types. Known uses: serves as a stimulant; assists aching muscles, headaches, anxious fatigue, and tension; help the flow of milk; stimulates hair; assists acne, professional athlete's foot, and open pores; and avoids the spread of contagious diseases. It likewise smells divine in soap.

Litseacubeba (Litseacubeba) A.k.a. May change. Antidepressant, antiseptic, astringent, insecticide Serves as a sedative; and helps indigestion, flatulence, lower back discomfort, chills, travel sickness, headaches, acne, oily skin, and extreme sweating,

Manuka (Leptospermum scoparium) Antibacterial, antifungal, and antiviral. Known uses: proven effective against both staph and strep infections. It's very comparable to the tea tree but smells much better. It can be made use of in place of tea tree.

Myrrh (Commiphora Myrrha) astringent, antiseptic, disinfectant, and deodorant. Known uses: Acts as a diuretic; promotes the immune system; helps gum conditions, sore throat, excessive mucus, colds, coughs, flatulence, hemorrhoids, wounds, weepy eczema, professional athlete's foot, jock itch, mouth ulcers, gingivitis, and bleeding or spongy gums. Do not use during pregnancy.

Myrtle (Myrtus Communis) Antiseptic, astringent, antibacterial, and expectorant. Known uses: Helps to deal with urinary and pulmonary infections, piles, sleeping disorders, and anxious conditions and acts as a sedative.

Neroli (Citrus aurantium) Antispasmatic, antidepressant, antibacterial, stimulant, and deodorant. Known uses: assists digestion, stress and anxiety, depression, stress, insomnia, damaged blood vessels, and oily or dry skin. Balances sebum.

Niaouli (Melaleuca quinquenervia) Antiseptic, antibacterial, decongestant, vermifuge, and insecticide. This is another form of melaleuca, and you can use it in place of tea tree oil. The Known uses: It helps to deal with head and chest colds and does not smell as bad as tea tree oil.

Oakmoss absolute (Evernia prunastri)

Characterized by its mossy, earthy and musky odor, oak moss's qualities are more spiritual and emotional than physical. It is soluble in alcohol and can be used as an anchor in most types of perfume. The Known uses: Can be used in fragrances and respiratory oils and eases busy sinuses.

Orange, bitter (Citrus sinensis) Antiseptic; originates from the peel of the orange. Known uses: help in calming, assists anxiety, is disinfecting, and is used in men's fragrances. Should be watered down before usage.

Oregano (Oreganum Vulgare) anti-inflammatory, Antibiotic, antioxidant, and expectorant. The Known uses: It helps infections; relieves pain, coughing, fever, and food digestion; counters effects of toxin; soothes muscle convulsions; and aids wounds.

Patchouli (Pogostemon patchouli) Antidepressant, antibacterial, astringent, antifungal, and insecticide. Understood uses: helps depression, injuries, acne, eczema, scars, cracked skin, fungal infections, scalp disorders, wrinkles, and cellulite; tightens up skin; and helps in tissue regeneration. Try blending with lemon, lime, or lavender essential oils for a fantastic aroma.

Peppermint (Menthe Piperita)   Decongestant, expectorant, and emmenagogue.

Known Uses: Helps to deal with pains, cramps, diarrhea, colic, nausea, swellings, joint pain, insect bites, acts as a stimulant, and helps itching or inflammation, and take a trip sickness. Avoid throughout pregnancy. When using soap, take care not to use excessively because it can cause a burning sensation in delicate areas.

.

CHAPTER THREE

Soap Molds

There's another essential piece of equipment you need if you're making bar soap, which's a soap mold. It's what brings everything together-- literally!

This chapter will focus on everything mold-related, from finding a mold-- or perhaps making your own-- to lining your frame to unmolding your finished soap.

What Can Be Used for a Soap Mold?

The more significant question is, what can't you use! Simply, about any container works as a soap mold-- other than anything metal, which would react with the lye and destroy your soap. We suggest you begin with a box or tray as your mold if you're a first-time soap-maker. You can even use a food storage container or buy the small 2-pound plastic tray mold that makes styles on the top of your soap bar. Some soap-makers use Pringle potato chip cans or PVC pipeline to make round soap bars. Shoeboxes can also be used.

You can discover many types of wooden, plastic, and acrylic molds in soap-making supply shops and online, in all sizes, from a 1-pound frame to as much as a 25-pound mold for the expert soap-makers. There are slab molds, upright molds, log molds, and trays. While you're going shopping, you're sure to come across log soap molds that have a soap bar cutter, divided molds that make ideal bars, and even molds with slits in the sides, so you can cut perfect bars with your soap knife. You'll discover no-liner frames and others that include premade liners; you just place up against the sides and bottom of the mold. Let's not forget about the individual plastic soap molds that make one bar at a time with a lovely design on the bar. Or a soap bar stamp! You can have them custom-made, for a reasonable cost so that you can stamp your logo or name on the top of every soap bar.

How To Make Your Own Soap Mold

To start, you'll need some wood. The easiest thing to do, if you do not have wood useful in the house, is to go to your local lumber shop and purchase either the precut5-inch- thick wood pieces near to the required sizes and after that complete them in your home, or have a store worker cut the pieces to the exact dimensions you need. Here's your wood list:.

- Two pieces each, 13 inches long, .5 inches thick and 2.5 inches large.
- Two pieces, each 11 inches long, .5 inch thick, and 2.5 inches broad.
- One piece 10 inches large and 12 inches long.

You'll also require the following:

- Wood glue.
- One little package of 1-inch nails.
- At least 2 C clamps.
- Hammer.
- Sandpaper.
- Varnish (optional).

This mold is about ten × 12 × 2 inches inside, holds 6.5 pounds (2,948.4 grams), and makes 16 bars of soap, each weighing about 6.5 ounces (184.3 grams). This shape mold is called a piece mold and is the simplest mold to use for doing swirls, embeds, and other fun and elegant styles.

Lining Your Mold.

Soap-makers often talk about utilizing everything from cling film to trash bags to line their molds, followed by the lament that they're always needing to combat having a smooth lining for a flat bar. And we've tried almost every method there is to line our soap molds, from making complex procurements and cutting out parts for the cornerstone the simple and easy technique we now make use of--white freezer paper.

We use freezer paper, shiny side up so that it won't stay with the soap. Making use of one large sheet and making folds and a slit in each corner, you, too, can line your mold in just a couple of minutes. There are no leakages since there are no cutouts and little, if any, waste. Freezer paper is readily offered, even in your grocery shop.

Here are steps to line your soap mold with freezer paper:

1. Step the length of your mold, and add 13 inches. The lining has to completely cover the within of your frame, up the sides and ends with a little extra for folding over each leading edge of the mold.

2. Lay the shiny side of the paper up, lengthwise next to your mold. Fold up one edge.

Line edge of the paper, which is folded against the inside side of your mold. With the use of your thumb, make a crease in the paper along with the other within the edge of the frame. After you've folded the second side, put the folded paper in your mold to be sure it fits efficiently and evenly.

3. Using the pointed part of your scissors, crease the paper properly where it butts up clearly and smoothly on each side. Fold and Crease down each end as you finished with the parties.

4. Working with one corner at a time, pull up the end piece while holding down the side piece, and crease the triangle fold, so it lies smooth and flat against the mold. Make a slit right in the corner edge of the paper. Now fold the paper properly over the edge on the end and tape it safely.

5. Fold the paper very well over the edges of the mold and tape securely. Inspect to be sure the lining is flat and still smooth.

See how easy that was? You'll be much more shocked how quickly your finished soap comes out of your freezer paper-- lined mold!

Melt-and-Pour Soap Molds.

There are lots of top quality plastic and silicone soap molds on the market designed for melt-and-pour (M&P) soap base. These molds do not have actually to be lined, but you might want to spray a cooking spray in the pattern before you pour in the M&P soap. You can likewise purchase a silicone spray mold release if you wish to-- lots of are offered online.

Your silicone mold can also be made by using a silicone item designed for that purpose. With one particular type, you paint the silicone over the thing you want to make a mold of. The type painted-on will not last through very many uses, but the other type will.

Unmolding Your Soap

Removing soap from the mold can be a discouraging experience depending on the type of image you're using, and whether or not you lined it, It doesn't matter if you've made use of M&P or made cold process soap; the very best way to get a stubborn soap out of the mold, specifically an unlined plastic tray or PVC pipe mold, is to put the filled shell in the freezer. Some will just require to be in the fridge for a few minutes, while others will need to be kept there overnight.

Depending on what kind of mold you're utilizing, you have some alternatives for getting rid of the soap.

Firstly, the process of removing soap from a plastic tray mold will be considered. When the soap is all set to come out of the freezer, you'll see that it has been withdrawn from the edges of the mold. Let the mold rest on a counter for about 5 minutes. Then, place a piece of waxed paper properly on your table, and after that, turn the soap tray upside down directly onto the paper. Next, gently press on the center of the back of the tray. You ought to have the ability to see the soap releasing from the mold. Continue to push till the soap pops entirely out of the frame. Allow the created soap to thaw to room temperature before cutting into bars if the tray is a slab type with bars.

Although the plastic no line Cold Process soap molds are very hassle-free molds to use, they can be tough to get rid of the soap from. However, if you use the freezer technique described previously in this section, you ought to be okay.

Lined molds are the most convenient type of pattern to remove your soap from. Loosen up the taped sides, turn the mold upside down on the waxed paper, and pull the mold straight up.

If you're utilizing a lined mold with knife slits, loosen the taped sides and, using your big soap knife, position the blade where it will fit into both slots, one on each side of the mold. Lay a piece of waxed paper properly on the counter, and turn your soap mold upside down. Then, remove the freezer paper gently from the cut bars of soap and be careful not to nick or bump the bars.

You are now all set to select the type of soap mold you want to try. Make sure to collect all the things you will require to utilize with your frame before you begin making your soap batch. Lining your mold initially is the most excellent method to begin. Don't wait until your soap is all set to be poured to line the image. Have it all set and waiting.

CHAPTER FOUR

The Basics of Cold Process Soap

Cold process (CP) soap is one approach of soap-making where the saponification happens in the mold. As earlier mentioned in this book, saponification is the chemical reaction of the lye connecting to the oils. This approach takes longer to cure.

Throughout this process, the soap batch goes through a boiling gel phase. After you've combined your oils and lye and brought the bunch to trace, you pour the soap into the mold, cover it with waxed paper, and walk away.

Saponification starts once the soap becomes strong

in the mold. Since it's hot and you can get lye burns on your fingers if you touch it, It is advisable not to move it.

Cold process soap maintains a creamier texture than hot process soap. As your experience with making soap increases, you might wish to attempt discounting the water stage to help speed up the curing. This isn't something advisable for a novice to try, however, so just attempt this approach after you've learned the ropes of soap-making. When you do, typically, the trace will come faster.

Soap is basically a wash-off product, and even though you'll get a few of the benefits by taking a bath instead of a shower, it all still just decreases the drain. Unless you're making a particular kind of bar designed for a specific reason, stick to the essential oils:

- Babassu oil.
- Castor oil.
- Coconut oil.
- Olive oil.
- Palm oil.
- Palm kernel oil.
- Peanut oil.
- Cocoa butter.
- Shea butter.

These will finish the job well and also keep the cost per bar affordable. If you desire a bit more conditioning, you can increase the extremely fat (oil that's not connected to lye),

Keep it basic. You do not need to add 1 ounce of this or 2 ounces of that in your batch to have a high bar of soap. Stick to the essentials, and your soap will be fantastic and cost-efficient.

One final tip: remember, always weigh your active ingredients instead of using volume measures such as tablespoons and cups. Much of the oils consider more than others, so if you utilize volume, you may have not adequate or too much lye. Be very precise when weigh- ing your components.

The Skinny on Super Fatting.

A lot of times we've heard new soap-makers-- and in some cases, even those more knowledgeable-- say "My soap is incredibly fatted with shea butter" or that their soap is very fatted with shea butter because they included it at trace.

When you're making cold process soap, this is clinically impossible. If you're making hot process soap, nevertheless, you can extremely fat after the cooking phase and right before the soap enters into the mold.

We pointed out super-fatting briefly in earlier chapters, but simply what is incredibly fatting? Fundamental chemistry tells you that in cold process soap, the lye does not understand the difference between the oils or when the oil/butter was added. All the butters and oils remain in the pot together. All the oil molecules join all the lye molecules. When all the lye particles.

Have connected to the oil molecules, what's left is the oil that's called the very fat. These unsaponified oil molecules provide additional conditioning for the skin. Including the oil or butter at trace does not keep that oil/butter from being saponified when making cold process since saponification happens over 48 hours.

Most soap-makers extremely fat at about 5 percent. In the winter period, you can raise it to about 8 percent to assist in combating winter dryness.

The Cold Process, Only Faster: Cold Process Oven Process.

The cold process oven process (CPOP) approach is perfect for those who remain in a rush to use or offer their soaps because it requires the gel phase and dries the soap faster-- sometimes in as low as 2 or 3 days, your solvents are harsh and prepared for usage. To make CPOP soap, merely follow the instructions for making regular cold process soap, other than put the soap-filled mold in the oven.

Here's how: right before you're prepared to begin mixing the lye and oils, preheat the oven to 170 ° F. Follow the directions for making CP soap, and pour your soap into the mold. Cover the top with waxed paper. Now shut off the oven, turn the oven light on, and put your pattern in the oven on the middle rack. Shut the door and leave it till the next day, take out the mold from the oven, let it stand a couple of hours to cool before you remove the soap from the shell, and sufficed into bars. Let the bars stay for a couple of days.

Unmolding and Cutting Your Soap.

Many individuals pick to unmold their soap batch after 24 hours; however, it appears this is too soon as the lye will still be active, and the soap will always be too soft. It's best to wait for about 48 hours before you take your soap out of the mold and set it on a drying rack.

When your soap is prepared, cover an area of your office with a piece of waxed paper. Loosen up the tape used to hold the freezer paper lining properly in place. Then, slowly move the soap onto the waxed paper. Let the soap dry for about a day or two before you try to suffice into bars.

Sally uses a ruler to the first process and mark the bars. The majority of soap-makers cut their bars about 2.25 inches wide and3.25 inches long.

Stand with the soap placed directly in front of you so you can push the cutter or knife straight down into the soap, making a tidy, straight cut. You may use a knife or handheld soap cutter to cut your soap,

Avoid trying to dry your soap in a humid area; rather than drying, they'll absorb the wetness in the air and end up being mushy.

Making Cold Process Soap.

Here are what you'll require:

- Stainless-steel stockpot.
- Several paper cups or measuring cups.
- Scale.
- Stainless-steel thermometer.
- Long-handled stainless-steel spoon.
- Thin latex gloves.
- Safety glasses.
- Freezer paper.
- Waxed paper.
- Soap mold.
- Paper towels.
- Skin-safe fragrance or essential oil.
- Soap-safe colorant.
- Oil(s).
- Sodium hydroxide lye.
- Distilled water.
- Stove.

Always take your recipe through a lye calculator before you become sure your lye and water phase are proper. This is a great routine to enter right from the start.

For every single pound of soap, you'll need 11 ounces of oils. The remainder of the pound comes from the lye and water. If you have a 3-pound mold, you'll require 33 ounces quantity of fats.

Basic Cold Process Soap

Here's what to put in SoapCalc:.

- Weight of Oils - 33 ounces.
- Water as % of Oils - 38.
- Super Fat % - 5.
- Fragrance Oz per Pound -.
- Pure water - (355.5 grams) 12.5 ounces
- Lye-- sodium hydroxide - (131.0 grams) 4.6 ounces
- Coconut oil - (76 degree) (187.1 grams) 6.6 ounces (20%).
- Castor oil - 187.1 grams (6.6 ounces) (20%).
- Palm oil - 561.3 grams (19.8 ounces) (60%).

Below are the specific soap qualities:

Hardness- 46

Cleansing -14

Conditioning -51

Bubbly -32

Creamy -50

Iodine -51

INS- 156

Consistently put on your gloves and shatterproof glass before you start:

1. Line the mold with freezer paper, following the instructions earlier provided in this book. If you're making use of a plastic tray mold, you don't require to line it.

2. Set your scale measurement to ounces (or grams if you so desire). Start pouring the water into the pitcher till it weighs 12.5 ounces (355.5 grams).

3. Place a bowl on the scale, push the tare button, and wait on the level to check out 0. With the use of a spoon or scoop, add the lye to the bowl till your scale checks out 4.6 ounces(131.0 grams). Take away the pan from the size.

4. Have the pitcher of water sitting in the sink or on a counter several inches away from you. Turn or open a near window on a drawing out fan. Slowly include the lye to the water and stir up until the lye is completely dissolved. You'll understand your lye is good since the water will end up being hot.

5. Keep the pitcher of lye/water in a safe location to cool off. This lasts about 1 hour.

6. Before you can proceed to weigh all your oils, the palm oil has to be melted and stirred simply because, just like milk, the palm oil separates. If you fail to melt and stir the oil properly, you'll get chalky white veins running on all your soap batch.

7. As soon as your palm oil has melted, and you've stirred it well, weigh 19.8 ounces (561.3 grams) on your scale and keep the oil in a stainless-steel container. Carry out the same process with the castor oil for 6.6 ounces (187.1 grams) and coconut oil for 6.6 ounces (187.1 grams).

8. Put on your security glasses and latex gloves once again.

9. When the oils and lye have cooled off to less than 90 ° F, it's time to make soap! Slowly put your lye/water service into your oils.

10. As soon as your oils are well blended with the lye water, it's time to include your fragrance.

11. Continue stirring up until you start to see the trace. This resembles the beginning of gravy or pudding, where you can see a little thickening as your spoon treads through the soap.

At this moment, if you have used a fast-moving or flower fragrance oil, put the batch into the mold. Otherwise, you have to continue stirring until you reach a medium trace and then put the soap into the prepared image.

Cover the soap's upper part with a piece of waxed paper. Leave the soap for 48 hours. The lye/water and oils are going through chemical modifications tooand these modifications are what make it soap as the lye particles connect to the soil particles.

Congratulations! You've just made your very first batch of soap.

Forty-eight hours later, your soap must be prepared to come out of the mold. Then, place a quantity of waxed paper on your counter, and thoroughly turn the soap mold upside down and place your soap on the paper.

Your soap will require time to cure so the water can vaporize and the bars harden. If you utilize your soap without it properly healing, it will melt quicker in the shower or bath.

The Zap Test

Before you utilize or give a fresh bar of soap, it's an excellent idea to be sure the lye has completely neutralized. This is where the zap test-- or the lick, yuck, and spit test-- is available inconvenient.

The test is easy: just touch the suggestion of your tongue to the bar of soap.

You could slip just one bar out of the batch to use after the soap has been sitting 3 or 4 days-- If you don't mind it melting in the water quicker, do the zap test! Absolutely nothing feels as high on your skin as hand- made soap. Once your family and pals discover out you're making soap, they'll all want to attempt a bar soap to share. Plus, it will provide you a terrific excuse to buy more scents! There's another dependency to contribute to the pot!

CHAPTER FIVE

Required some soap quickly but don't wish to wait 2 to 4 weeks for the soap to cure? Hot process soap requires little to no cure time!

The Basics of Hot Process Soap

Hot process soap-making is a technique of cooking the soap mix on the range up until it has finished saponifying (made into soap). When the solvent has ended up cooking and has cooled, it's all set to utilize. With the use of this process, you can add oils after the cooking stage to high fat since the

The saponification process has currently consumed all the lye. Hot process soap-making does not make as quite a bar of soap as cold process soap; however, it does offer pleasure principle!

There's a new method to make hot process soap. You begin with cold process soap, and after putting the detergent into the mold, place it in an oven preheated to 170 ° F. Allow the soap to prepare at this temperature for 4 hours, shut off the heat, and leave the mold in the oven up until it has cooled off. When you take it out of the oven, it's prepared to cut and utilize. The heat of the stove requires the soap into saponification and holds it there for a few hours. With this approach, you have the beauty of cold process soap and the no-wait of the hot process soap-- the best of both worlds!

The one downside to hot process soap is that it's challenging to get out of the mold. There's an easy fix for that: line your mold with freezer paper, with the bright side against the soap. Your soap will come out of the shell with ease.

Making Hot Process Soap

Before we begin, make sure you have whatever you require at hand. You won't have much time to go around looking for things you've forgotten when things get started. Here's what you'll need:

- Face shield or Safety glasses.
- Plastic pitcher.
- Scale.
- Thin latex gloves.
- Glass or Plasticcereal bowl and one small glass or stainless-steel cup.
- One stainless-steel or 2-cup determining cup or glass bowl.

- Long-handled stainless-steel spoon or plastic spoon.
- Large stainless-steel (stock) pot.
- Immersion blender.
- Mold lined with freezer paper.
- Stove with an oven.

The recipe provided in this section is necessary; however, any method will do if you wish to try something entirely different.

Standard Hot Process Soap.

This is a hard type of soap. The cleansing process is mild, and the conditioning is a little bit low, however, putting 8 percent in the super fat instead of 5 percent enhances the conditioning. With a combined bubbly and creamy lather quantities, at 67, this soap produces loads of soap. This recipe is capable of making a total of 17.11 ounces (about 485.1 grams) of soap.

Here's what to put in SoapCalc:.

- Weight of Oils -11 ounces.
- Super Fat % 8.
- Water as % of Oils - 38.
- Distilled water 4.18 ounces (about 118.503 grams).
- Fragrance Oz per Lb.7.

- Lye-- salt hydroxide 1.454 ounces (about 41.232 grams).

- Coconut oil.88 ounce (about 24.948 grams) (8%).

- Olive oil 1.10 ounces (about 31.185 grams) (10%).

- Beef tallow 7.92 ounces (about 224.532 grams) (72%).

- Castor oil 1.10 ounces (about 31.185 grams) (10%).

- Fragrance oil.481 ounce (about 13.640 grams).

Now is the time to get it all set if you want to add a colorant to your soap. Step the maker's advised use amount for the size of soap batch you're making, and pour it in the stainless-steel bowl or 2-cup measuring cup. If you're making use of a powder colorant, you need to include a little oil to wet the dye so it will be all set when it's time to color. (See Chapter 11 for more details on utilizing colorants.).

Here are the soap qualities:.

- Hardness - 50.

- Cleansing - 11.

- Conditioning - 48.

- Bubbly - 20.

- Creamy - 47.

- Iodine - 50.

- INS - 146.

Before we go any even more, let's discuss dishes a little bit more, especially the portions used in them. If you get a recipe that just lists pieces for the, do not freak out.

Using portions for a recipe makes it extremely simple to size up or size down the soap batch to fit the mold you want to utilize. For every single pound of soap, it takes 11 ounces oil and 5 ounces water/lye option. Click Calculate Recipe, and SoapCalc transforms the recipe to fit your soap mold.

You can likewise increase the percentage of the oil by the quantity of the overall weight of oils for the size batch you desire. For one pound batch, you need about 11 ounces of oil. If the palm oil is 72, boost by 11 (the number of fats you're going to make use of), and you get7.92 ounces (224.5 grams). Easy! If you desire to make 2 pounds of soap, increase all the parts in the recipe by 22, the ounces of oils, it takes to make two pounds of soap. To be sure, your calculation is right, including all the ounces, and you need to have either11 ounces (for about 1 pound of soap) or 22 ounces (which is about 2 pounds of soap).

Continuously put on your gloves and safety glasses before you begin.

1. Line your mold with freezer paper (glossy side up), following the directions in earlier. If you're using a plastic tray mold, you do not have to line it.

2. Ensure you set your scale to ounces (or grams if you're an international reader). Place the ceramic bowl on the size, and press the tare button to zero out the weight of the cup, and await the scale to read 0. Start putting the fragrance oil into the bowl up until it weighs—481 ounce (13.640 grams). Get rid of the pan from the scale, and set it aside in the meantime.

3. Do the same for the colorant, and reserved.

4. Place a cereal bowl-- size bowl on the scale, and press the tare button to zero out the weight of the container. Weigh each oil individually and include it to the stockpot.

5. Ensure you place the stockpot of oils over medium-low heat. Let the oils completely melt.

6. Place on your shatterproof glass and latex gloves again.

7. As the oils are heating up, put a plastic bowl on the scale, and press the tare button to zero out the weight of the container. Weigh the salt hydroxide (lye) in the box. Then, eliminate the bowl from the scale and set it aside.

8. Place a pitcher on the scale, and press the tare button to zero out the weight of the pitcher. Weigh the distilled water. Get rid of the pitcher from the level, and set it aside.

9. When the oils have entirely melted, it's time to blend your lye into the water.

Put on your security glasses and latex gloves once again. Now gradually spray the lye into the water, stirring while you do this and keeping your face away from the pitcher until all the lye has liquified.

Remember, the fumes from the lye can burn your eyes and lungs, so don't get your face too close to that pitcher!

10. With the pot still over medium-low heat, gradually put the lye/water mixture into the oils. Using an immersion mixer, mix till the oils and water come together.

11. Continue to stir, with the pot on the heat, as the soap begins concerning trace.

12. The soap will then go through the next stage. This is the moment the soap looks like it is falling apart; however, it's expected to do this. The soap is going through the gel and is saponifying.

13. Continue with the cooking, although the applesauce phase. It will saponify and then start to smooth out. This is the "mashed potato" phase, and now is the time to include the fragrance and color. Add your fragrance first and stir up until it's well mixed. The amount of coloring you use depends on how dark or light you want the completed soap to be. Using your long-handled spoon, dig about 1 cup (8 ounces) of the soap and add it to the bowl with the colorant. Stir well till the mix forms one uniform color. Then, add the colored soap back into the pot, and stir in

the shade until you have the preferred effect-- less stirring offers you a two-colored, swirled bar; the more you stir, the more you get one color. Take out another cup of soap and add more color if the color is too light. Stir it well and take back to the soap pot. You do have to work rapidly before the soap batch starts establishing.

Put the soap into the freezer paper-- lined mold. Now let the soap cool off. You can then leave your soap to cool on your counter or put it in a cold oven, with the oven door somewhat left open, so the soap is out of the way.

You'll require a soap cutter or a long knife. Put your cutter over the very first cutting line and push strongly directly down all the way through the soap.

Making Slow Cooker Hot Process Soap.

It's just as quick and easy as making soap on the range. The only difference is your range and stockpot are complimentary for simmering a pot of stew while you make soap in your slower cooker. After taking dinner, you could relax in a high hot bath using a bar of your newly formed soap! That's the best ending to a busy day if you ask me.

In addition to the majority of the tools noted earlier in the "Making Hot Process Soap" area, you will need a good-quality slow cooker. Some have two temperature level settings (high and low), and some have three (low, medium, and high). It is advisable to use a slow cooker with three settings, because the one having two settings becomes too hot when set on a low level.

Slow Cooker Hot Process Soap

The natural, hands-off recipe can yield 17.2 ounces (487.6 grams) of soap.

Here's what to put in SoapCalc:.

- Water as % of Oils - 38
- Weight of Oils - 11 ounces.
- Super Fat % - 8
- Fragrance Oz per Lb. - 07.
- Distilled water - 118.501 grams (4.18 ounces)
- Lye-- salt hydroxide - 42.455 grams (1.498 ounces).
- Palm oil - 224.528 grams (7.92 ounces) (72%).
- Castor oil - 31.184 grams (1.10 ounces) (10%)
- Coconut oil - 56.132 grams (1.98 ounces) (18%).
- Fragrance oil - 481 ounce (13.64 grams) (.7%).

Here are the soap qualities:.

- Hardness- 50.
- Cleansing - 13.
- Conditioning - 47.
- Bubbly - 22.
- Creamy - 46.
- Iodine - 49
- INS - 160.

Ensure you always wear your gloves and safety glasses before you begin.

1. Line your mold with freezer paper (glossy side up), following the directions earlier mentioned. If you're using a plastic tray mold, you do not require to lining it, but it can be helpful if you spray the frame using a cooking oil spray.

2. Place a ceramic bowl properly on the scale, and then push the tare button to zero out the weight of the pan eventually. Measure the importance of the fragrance oil and then set it aside.

3. Take the same step for the colorant, and set aside.

4. Heat the slow cooker to high.

5. Place a cereal bowl-- size bowl on the scale, and push the tare button to zero out the weight of the container. Weigh each oil individually and contribute to the slow cooker.

6. Put on your security glasses and latex gloves once again.

7. When the oils are heating up, put a plastic bowl on the scale, and push the tare button to zero out the weight of the container. Weigh the sodium hydroxide in the box. Take off the bowl from the scale, and set it aside.

8. Place a pitcher on the scale, and press the tare button to zero out the weight of the pitcher. Weigh the distilled water. Get rid of the pitcher from the size and set aside.

9. When all the oils have melted, it's time to blend the water and lye. Slowly add up the lye to the water and stir with a long spoon. Stir the mixture up until all the lye has been dissolved.

10. Slowly put the lye/water mix into the slow cooker. Using an immersion blender, blend till the soap concerns trace/starts to thicken. This may take 10 to 15 minutes. Once it has begun to trace, stop mixing, turn the heat to low, and place it on the cover. Allow it to rest for a while as you take the next action.

11. Put some of the oxides/glycerin solution into a bowl. Dry oxides can also work-- simply blend your dry oxides with the glycerin. I can't tell you how much to begin with; this is an experimental thing.

12. This is the particular stage when your soap will begin to separate, and oil will start coming to the top. Do not stress-- this becomes part of the gel stage, and it's supposed to do this. Keep stirring! The soap might attempt to climb up out of the pot or

boil over if you don't keep stirring. You can turn off the heat once you reach the mashed potato stage. Stir the soap while it cools off some. If your slow cooker is the type that can be removed from the base, transfer it to help the soap cool off a little faster.

13. When the soap has cooled off, add the fragrance oil, and ensure you mix well enough. Using your long spoon, scoop out about 1 cup soap and add it to the bowl with the colorant. Stir well until the dye is incorporated. Then, add the colored soap back to the pan, and stir in the color till you have the desired impact-- less stirring provides you a two-colored, swirled bar; the more you stir, the more you get one color.

14. Put the soap into the freezer paper-- lined mold.

Smooth down the top as much as you can. Bang the mold on the counter a couple of times to allow the air bubbles to get out. Let the soap cool off completely. You can keep the soap mold on your kitchen counter while it cools off or put it in a cold oven to get it out of the way. Then, cut into bars, after which your soap is ready to use.

Making Cold Process Oven Process Soap

The Cold process oven process (CPOP), hot process oven process (HPOP), in the mold oven process (ITMOP)-- whatever you call it, you're saying the same thing:

It's the cold process soap put in the oven to give room for the gel phase and speed up the process of saponification. It's the best of both worlds-- the smoothness of cold process soap without the cure time.

In addition to the majority of the tools listed previously in the "Making Hot Process Soap" section, you would also need an acrylic mold if you choose to only utilize the oven light for heat. Make sure to line your mold.

The recipes presented in this section are capable of making approximately 1 pound of soap. The very first one has a cleansing of 13, the second one has a cleansing of 11, and the 3rd has a cleansing of 8. The 13 is best matched for the healthy skin, while the eight works better for dry skin.

Cold Process Oven Process Soap Used for Normal Skin

The recipe can yield about 17.2 ounces (487.6 grams) of soap.

Here's what to put in SoapCalc:

- Weight of Oils - 11 ounces

- Water as % of Oils - 38

- Super Fat % - 8

- Fragrance Oz per Pound - .07

- Pure water- 118.501 grams (4.180 ounces).

- Lye-- salt hydroxide - 42.455 grams (1.498 ounces).

- Palm oil - 224.528 grams (7.92 ounces) (72%).

- Castor oil - 31.184 grams (1.10 ounces) (10%).

- Coconut oil - 56.132 grams (1.98 ounces) (18%).

- Fragrance oil - 13.64 grams (481 ounce) (.7%).

Here are the soap qualities:.

Hardness- 50.

Cleansing - 13.

Conditioning - 47.

Bubbly - 22

Creamy - 46.

Iodine - 49.

You'll begin this soap on the stove and complete it in the oven. There are two options for the heat: you can either turn on the light in the oven before you begin measuring out the oils or preheat the oven to 170 ° F. Always put on your gloves and safety glasses before you start.

Directions

1. Line your mold correctly with freezer paper (shiny side up). If you're utilizing a plastic tray mold, you do not require to line it.

2. Put the plastic pitcher properly on the scale, and press the tare button to zero out the weight of the pitcher. Pour the precise quantity of water stated in the recipe requirements into the pitcher, and then set it aside.

3. Put the plastic bowl properly on the scale and weigh out the precise amount of lye stated in the recipe requirements.

4. Pour the lye into the water contained in the pitcher and stir up until completely dissolved. You will not utilize this up until it has cooled off.

5. Measure the weight of all the oils on the scale and carefully add them to the pot. You can go ahead to stir at this point if you want, but you do not need to. Set over low heat, and permit the oils to melt. Do not let them get too hot. We usually leave a few

of the coconut or palm unmelted. (The oils will be warm adequate to continue melting the bit that hasn't melted after you get rid of the pot from the heat. And this way, you do not need to wait as long.)

6. Measure the weight of the fragrance oil already in the bowl, and then set it aside.

7. When the lye/water and oil have cooled down, put the fragrance oil into the other oils. Pour the lye/water into the oils, and ensure you stir with whisk or spoon. Pour the soap properly into the mold and use a spatula to get all the soap out of the pot when you see the light trace.

8. If you're using a wood mold, place it on the leading shelf of the oven, and then close the oven door. Leave the oven to be on for about two hours and then turn it off, leaving the soap alone, inside the closed oven, until the next morning. Avoid opening the oven door!

9. Remove the hot mold from the oven, and let it cool off. Get rid of the soap from the image, cut it, and it's all set to be used.

Cold Process Oven Process Soap for a Mild Skin.

This is one of our preferred recipes. The recipe can be made to fit your soap mold using the quantity listed beside each oil. This recipe can yield 17.3 ounces (490.5 grams) of soap.

Here's what to put in SoapCalc:.

- Weight of Oils - 11 ounces.

- Water as % of Oils - 38.

- Super Fat % - 8.

- Fragrance Oz per Pound - 7.

- Distilled water- 118.501 grams (4.180 ounces).

- Lye-- sodium hydroxide - 42.099 grams (1.485 ounces).

- Coconut oil - 46.777 grams (1.65 ounces) (15%).

- Palm oil - 233.883 grams (8.25 ounces) (75%).

- Fragrance - 481 ounce (13.64 grams).

- Castor oil - 31.184 grams (1.10 ounces) (10%).

Here are the soap qualities:.

- Hardness - 49.
- Cleansing - 11.
- Conditioning - 48.
- Bubbly lather - 20.
- Velvety lather - 48.
- Iodine - 50.
- INS157.

Cold Process Oven Process Soap Used for Sensitive Skin.

This moderate soap is perfect for those of you who have delicate skin. This recipe can yield17.2 ounces (487.6 grams) of soap.

Here's what to put in SoapCalc:.

- Weight of Oils - 11 ounces.
- Water as % of Oils - 38.
- Super Fat % - 8.
- Fragrance Oz per Pound - 7.
- Pure water - 4.180 ounces (118.501 grams).
- Lye-- salt hydroxide - 41.505 grams (1.464 ounces).
- Coconut oil - 31.184 grams (1.1 ounces) (10%).
- Palm oil - 249.476 grams (8.8 ounces) (80%).

- Castor oil- 31.184 grams (1.1 ounces) (10%).

- Fragrance oil- 13.640 grams (.481 ounce) (.7%).

Here are the soap qualities:.

- Hardness - 48.

- Cleansing - 8.

- Conditioning - 50.

- Bubbly - 17.

- Creamy - 49.

- Iodine - 52.

- INS - 151.

This type of recipe is even a little milder than the preceding two. The more delicate the skin, the lower the cleaning requirements to be.

Prepare as earlier recommended for Cold Process Oven Process Soap for NormalSkin recipe.

Cold Process Oven Process Soap for Hard Skin.

This soap is fantastic for eczema or for pets who fume areas in the summer season. This recipe yields about482 grams(17 ounces) soap.

Below are what to put in SoapCalc:.

- Water as % of Oils - 38.

- Weight of Oils - 11 ounces.

- Fragrance Oz per Lb - 5

- Super Fat % - 5.

- Distilled water- 118.501 grams (4.18 ounces).

- Lye-- salt hydroxide - 41.102 grams (1.45 ounces).

- Palm oil - 187.107 grams (6.6 ounces) (60%).

- Coconut oil- 31.184 grams (1.1 ounces) (10%).

- Karanja oil - 31.184 grams (1.1 ounces) (10%).

- Neem oil - 31.184 grams (1.1 ounces) (10%).

- Castor oil - 31.184 grams (1.1 ounces) (10%).

- Juniper essential oil- 9.750 grams (.34 ounce).

Here are the soap qualities:.

- Hardness - 42.
- Cleansing - 7.
- Conditioning - 54.

- Bubbly - 16.

- Creamy - 44.

- Iodine - 59.

- INS - 149.

This soap will become a little soft, but it'll harden up in a couple of days.

Prepare as advised for the previous Cold Process Oven Process Soap for NormalSkin recipe.

CHAPTER SIX

What Are Bath Bombs?

It is essential to find the best things to take care of yourself when it comes to taking care of your health. Whether you are looking to keep yourself tidy, provide yourself with a little relaxation and self-care, or you want to produce a medication that is going to make you feel healthier than before, you need to discover the products that are the very best for you and will be healthy and natural for your body.

The problem for a lot of individuals is that the products that they use in and on their bodies are not often safe. You will discover that the medications, hair shampoos, creams and conditioners, and lots more have lots of chemicals, and the majority of them have components that you aren't even able to pronounce much less something that you can also understand. This can be harmful; if you don't know the item that you are placing on or in your body, how do you know if it is safe for you to use?

This explains why there has been such a move over to making some homemade products for beauty and health. People are making, and some are offering to others who don't have the time to do this, various products such as body lotions, face creams, medicines, and so far more. These are often made with just a couple of active ingredients, many of which you will be able to pronounce, and the elements are discovered in nature, so you understand that they are great for you. These assist you in avoiding all the problems that come with those chemicals that can be found in many health and beauty products and you can choose the type that is going to work out the best for you; selecting the color, shape, quantity, and even scent or taste that goes with them.

Bath bombs are one of the products that you can pick from when it has to do with making some of these items on your own. These are tiny balls of soap that you will have the ability to add to your bathwater. You can sort of see them like your soap or bubble bath, and they are going to help you to get your skin beautiful and tidy in the tub. If you add some of the ideal components, such as a particular type of essential oils, you will find that they can help with skin problems, relaxation, and other concerns that you are attempting to solve.

While there exist many different recipes that you will have the ability to pick from when making your bath bomb, and you can make a considerable variation based on what you are trying to heal on the body or your personal choice, the majority of them are going to be created with citric acid and baking soda. Both of these are going to respond in the water in such a way that they will offer you some bubbles and an excellent fizzing noise, which provides their name.

There are a lot of reasons to use a bath bomb. Some parents like to use these for their children to assist make bath time more enjoyable while adding in some lavender or other scents to soothe them down at the end of the night. It can also contribute to supply more moisture to the skin and aid kids with different skin or health concerns, without needing to use damaging chemicals and medications to treat these concerns.

Adults are going to find that the bath bombs are handy too. These bath bombs can be used to add more energy to cure skin issues, to assist with relaxation, and so far more. They are simple to make, and if you select the right type of essential oils, you will be able to make a wide range of them and make them in your own home without excessive trouble. We will offer some terrific recipes that you can use when you are very first starting with using this product.

The main point that comes behind using the bath bombs is to use aromatherapy. While you can definitely pick to go with a bath bomb that is not loaded with essential oils and you would still feel clean and get a few of the advantages, the significant benefits are going to come when you can include some essential oils to help you out. These are the particular things that are going to assist you in getting relaxed, feel more stimulated, or dealing with some other condition that you are trying to work on.

Aromatherapy is a process that has been around for several years. It has frequently been used as a source of medication, and often it is chosen because it allows you to enjoy the health gain from a product that originates from nature rather than relying on one that is made in a factory or another lab and has absolutely nothing natural within it.

The oils that are utilized in aromatherapy all have various sorts of active ingredients inside that are suggested to assist the body in a natural method, and therefore it is so much better. Using an essential oil like lavender can help you to feel relaxed, and one like lemon oil will assist in revitalizing you and making you feel much better than ever before because of the effect that these have on your body and your mind.

To get the benefits of the aromatherapy into your bath, you just need to include a couple of drops of the essential oil into your bath bomb. Then when you are taking a shower, simply add in the weapon, let it have a few minutes to liquefy, and after that, simply sit back and unwind. The scents are going to go through the air, assisting you to receive the advantages of aromatherapy simply while cleaning and relaxing off in the bath. Besides, all those skin-friendly ingredients are going to go all around the bathwater, assisting in keeping the skin tidy and clean and helping out in so many ways.

Whether you acquire these bath bombs from somebody else or you select to make them by yourself, you will find that it is easy to discover them in the fragrance, color, and style that you desire. So you can pick one that is going to raise your mood and spirits if this is the issue that you are dealing with, or you can use them to help you to relax and unwind down before going to sleep. All in all, these are the finest and the all-natural method to help you to get precisely what your body needs, all from a little bath bomb that enters into your bathwater.

No one would have thought that such a simple thing could make such a massive difference in your body and with your mind? These bombs are often just going to have a few active ingredients, but you will find that after using them for a brief amount of time, they are going to become your favorite part of the entire day.

CHAPTER SEVEN

Homemade Bath Bombs

There is nothing much better than taking in a hot bath and the pressure escaping away. If this is your concept of nirvana, then a moisturizing and aromatic bath bomb will take this pleasure to the next level. Not just will you get the physical and psychological release, but bath bombs appeal to your sense of smell, offering you a new sensory experience.

It is difficult not to like bath bombs. The sensation of bathing in them is incredibly like bathing in champagne. The carbonated bubbles that they produce can not put a smile but help on your face. This is the reason that they are a lot of fun, how they take the experience to an entirely new level.

When you have gained a little experience with store-bought bath bombs, and you have a better concept of the types of essential oils and fragrances that you would like to utilize, it is time to take the next action: making your own bath bombs. It might sound harsh, but in reality, it is rather easy. All you would have to do is take some necessary steps.

Among the immediate benefits of making your bath bombs is the safe inexpensive; it is much more costly to buy them than to acquire the couple of components that you will need to make your own. In a short time, you will be having your own exciting health club day at home with your homemade bath bombs.

To make your bath bombs, you will require the following ingredients.

- Sodium bicarbonate
- Citric acid
- Epsom salt
- Water
- Olive or coconut oil
- Food coloring (your preference).
- Essential oil (with a scent that you enjoy, along with the advantages that you are searching for).

Step One.

Mix the baking soda with the Epsom salt and the citric acid in a ratio of 2 to 1. I would start with two cups of baking soda and mix in a bowl each of citric acid powder and Epsom salt.

Step Two.

In another bowl, we are going to mix the wet active ingredients. We want to begin with four tablespoons of either coconut or olive oil. This will keep your bath bomb from being a dud once it hits the water for the first time. You desire to include two tablespoons of the essential oil that you selected. Now you should have the aroma that you were looking for your bath bomb.

You would scrap it and start over if it doesn't smell like what you desire. Perhaps choose a different oil, if possible. Just keep in mind that what you feel is what you will get.

Step Three.

Now you wish to blend the wet ingredients into your dry ingredients. You would have to do this gradually. I recommend doing it at a tablespoon at a time, to prevent the mixture fizzing too early. If it does fizz excessive, there is no embarrassment to start over and attempt again.

Throughout this stage of blending the wet ingredients with the dry ones, you can add a few drops of your favored food coloring. Put it in after you have integrated the parts, but before you have begun whisking whatever together. Blend thoroughly, blending everything well. Your last mixture must have no dry crumbs in it and need to be combined regularly throughout. Do not hesitate to utilize your hands to squish the mix, if required, to eliminate these last little bits of crumbs.

Step Four.

Take whatever you wish to make use of as a mold. This could be as little as a cup. You want to grease the frame with a couple of drops of olive or coconut oil and spread it around regularly. Next, you wish to take your bath bomb mix and pack it into the mold, pushing down securely on it to get out any excess air.

Step Five.

Typically let the mold set for fifteen minutes, then thoroughly take the bath bomb out of the image, squeezing gently on it to shape the sides properly. If you are having a hard time keeping it together, reinsert it in the mold, pressing down firmly and let it sit for another fifteen minutes. Then attempt this removal process all over again.

Step Six.

At this point, our objective is to try and remove as much of the excess liquid as possible. An excellent method to do this is to gently pat down the bath bomb with a paper towel to absorb some of the residual wetness. Do not fret about attempting to get too much out of it; the majority of moisture will ultimately dry off. I then take an airtight container and place the bath bomb in it. I will then save it in a cool location for a minimum of three days, at which point there needs to be no residual moisture in the bath bomb.

Now that does not seem so bad, right? While making homemade bath bombs is a simple process, you might discover yourself having to do it a couple of times initially up until you master it. Do not give up if your first effort does not prosper. Sometimes you have to go through the process a few times actually to comprehend how everything works.

CHAPTER EIGHT

The advantages of Making Your Bath Bombs

Now, when you are selecting out whether you wish to use bath bombs, you have two options. You can choose to go on the internet and order the bath bombs that you would be able to use in your own home. There are a lot of people who delight in making these at home and will offer them on sites, such as Etsy and more. Another choice is to make some on your own, where you can choose the ingredients and all the other things that you take into your bath bomb.

Making the bath bomb at home is one of the best choices. Let's consider some of the reasons that you would choose to make these bath bombs on your own.

Choosing the ingredients

When you go to the shop to choose some of the products that you wish to use, you may be astonished at the absence of options. There aren't numerous options in terms of colors, aromas, ingredients, and more. Besides, most of the items on the racks have plenty of harmful chemicals that are bad on the whole body rather than the all-natural components that you can find inside homemade bath bombs. If you are trying to cut out some of the chemicals that are in your items or you have some allergies you require to be careful of, you will take pleasure in that you get to supervise the active ingredients that are inside the bath bomb. Even if you aren't fussy since you do not have allergic reactions, it is still good to have an idea of the specific ingredients that remain in the products you use on your body.

More affordable

Making your homemade bath bombs at home can be cost-effective. There are a lot of products that are on the shelves at your store, but most of them are going to be pretty expensive. You will be shocked at how a couple of components are in most of the bath bombs that you are making, and because you are creating them in bulk, you are going to get a heap of items for a meager price. Lots of individuals who are looking to save cash, as well as guaranteeing that they are getting an all-natural and healthy item, will change over to making their bath bombs to get those savings they are looking for.

Avoid bad chemicals

One of the crucial reasons that people will start to take a look at making bath bombs, as well as a few of the other homemade health and beauty products, is since they are tired of all the harmful chemicals that they are dealing with within their routine products. These chemicals have been revealed male times to be bad for the body, making it difficult to remain healthy and triggering more harm than excellent. When you make some of your bath bombs in the house, you will find that you can prevent a few of the harmful chemicals that are around you, and instead you can concentrate on including 100% natural products that will help keep your skin healthy and clean.

Get the choice of what you use

If you would like to have a particular color with the bath bomb, you can make them that method. You are the one who will pick what goes inside the bath bomb and what you are going to get out of the end item.

Get innovative

There is a lot of imagination that comes with producing your bath bomb. Try out a lot of different essential oils and find out which one you are going to like the most.

Blending some colors to get something new. Some bath bombs will have little presents that are inside, various colors, and something else that is unique. If you need some more ideas of what you can make with your bath bomb, have a look at some of the ideas that are online and attempt a few of them out.

Great ideas for gifting

Homemade gifts are often some of the very best tips. They reveal the other individual that you appreciate them and that you can make it distinct to the person that you are intending on providing the homemade present to. Nothing is much better than utilizing a bath bomb as a gift to somebody you love. You will be able to include the scents that work for you, the colors, and so far more. Produce a great little box to hold the bath bombs and decorate it also. What is better than a present that is from the heart that will assist in relaxing and reviving the individual you love, which reveals a little bit of imagination!

An excellent family activity

You can allow the kids to have some of the active ingredients and even the choice of which essential oils they would like to put into their bath bombs. Kids will take pleasure in all the mixing, picking the fragrances and putting the weapons together, and you can get it all done while keeping them captivated on the weekend, during cold and snowy days, or throughout breaks.

Make in big batches

When you are making some of your bath bombs, you will be the one that is in control of how many that you make. Making these bath bombs at house enables you to truly get a good stock going, enough to last some time, and even adequate to have a bath bomb each night of the week.

Making a bath bomb in the house is among the very best concepts that you can do. Not just will you get some of the excellent benefits that have been promised in this manual, you can also utilize some of your imagination to have some enjoyable and make the ideal bath bomb for all your needs. See some of the advantages of making these by yourself and home and see how fantastic it can be!

Uses for Your Bath Bombs

When you initially become aware of bath bombs, you might be a bit curious as to how they are going to work and if you are going to get some benefits out of using these. Many people assume that they are a silly little thing that you can include in your bath and that they can be enjoyable, but there is a lot more that is going to include these bath bombs, and there are also many benefits that you can take pleasure in. A few of the great things that you can do with your bath bombs consist of:

Skin conditioning

Among the very first reasons that you would utilize these bath bombs is to help to soften and even condition your skin. Often your skin is going to get rough. Maybe you have skin that has trouble keeping the moisture, and in some cases, the bad weather condition throughout the winter season can make it hard for the skin to remain soft and high. You can quickly add in the right oils in addition to some vitamin E oil to your bath bomb and then soak for a bit to get all the skincare benefits that you are trying to find.

In addition to helping to make the skin a bit softer, you are going to delight in that these bath bombs can aid with firming up the loose skin to eliminate unpleasant skin marks. You can add in some coconut oil to the bath bomb to help renew moisture in the skin. If you are dealing with skin that is oily, you should think about utilizing a bath bomb that has some tea tree oil because it is going to drag out a few of the oils that are on the skin, while not drying it out too much like some other harsh chemicals will do.

Hair Conditioning

If you need some aid with washing your hair and you can't find that 100% natural hair shampoo that you wish to utilize, then bath bombs are going to supply you with the help that you need. There are numerous dishes that you can select, which can assist you in getting your hair to be shiny and soft. Rosemary and thyme are going to help the most with your hair. If you are having some issues with dandruff on the nose, you ought to utilize tea tree oil. Lavender can assist in making the hair soft and high in addition to a floral odor.

Stress relief

One of the main reasons that many people choose to opt for bath bombs is to help them get some stress and anxiety relief. Bath bombs are simple to make and easy to make use of. With the help of some crucial essential oils, including cherry blossom, orange, vanilla, geranium, and cedar, they are going to help you decrease the stress and anxiety and stress in your body and those that are going to help you to deal with your tension.

Lavender and some other relaxing ones can help to make you feel much better than ever in the past because they will assist not only to get rid of some of the tension, but a few of their properties benefit those having symptoms of depression and more.

Cold relief.

Another reason that you might decide to make a bath bomb is to help out with some sinus concerns that feature a terrible cold. Eucalyptus oil can be included in the bath bomb to assist drain out the sinuses, and clove oil is going to help out well. Just add these essential oils into the bath bomb, location it into your bath, and simply soak for about twenty minutes or so, allowing the sinuses to clear out while you sit back and inhale all the sweet fragrances that come from utilizing the essential oils.

Sprains

There are times when you are going to deal with ligament problems, sprains, and other concerns with the muscles. You will discover that these problems are going to get worse if you are active or you have an abnormally hectic day. There is a great solution that you can utilize that will help supply relief that is practically immediate and is much more secure than taking any of the painkillers that are out there.

If you are dealing with some of these muscles and sprains problems, you must consider making a bath bomb that has peppermint, ginger, and rosemary. All of these have a lot of advantages that will help to unwind and reduce the pain all the muscle discomforts that you are dealing with, and you can get rid of concerns like convulsions, strains,

and sprains. All you will need to do to get these benefits is add in a bath bomb to the water that you are utilizing for a bath. If you need a great deal of additional power in the bath bomb, think about including some water into a pail and then positioning the bath bomb inside to get the same impact.

Cleaners

Not just are you able to position the bath bomb into your bathwater, but you will likewise have the ability to place it into other kinds of water and use them as a way to tidy up your home. There are a couple of essential oils that are wonderful for cleaning up the house. Eucalyptus oil is fantastic for helping to clean up the flooring and will help to include an additional shine to the floor while also dealing with some issues with mosquitos. You can likewise make one with lavender oil to get rid of the musty odor that is in your carpets.

You will be able to make a great deal of various solutions to the bath bombs based on what you would like to tidy up in your home. There is a need to have a look at the distinct residential or commercial properties that remain in the essential oil and see if it is going to clean up the necessary things that you are attempting to work on. Practically any essential oil is going to work inside the bath bombs, so you will be able to mix and match them to get the outcomes that you require for cleaning your home.

For your family pets

To end this out, you are likewise able to use the bath bombs to assist your animals. Adding some clove oil to a bath bomb and after that, washing your pet with this mix will help to eliminate fleas and ticks on your animal. You can include a bit of vitamin e oil to soften up the coat of the family pet. One thing to keep in mind is to evaluate out a little the oil on the family pet first, in a localized area, to make sure that they can handle it, and you will not have them with an allergy when using the product. Some cats are going to be sensitive to these. Still, because you are utilizing essential oils on the animals and these are natural, there usually isn't going to be excessive of a problem with these.

As you can see, there are a lot of fantastic advantages that you are going to be able to delight in when you choose to deal with bath bombs. These bath bombs are all-natural and full of healthy components that benefit the body. You will be able to select the essential oil that you wish to include into the bath bomb to assist raise your mood, deal with sprains and pressures, aid to clear off the skin, and so much more. You get to be in charge of the components that come into your bath bomb, and you are sure to find the results that will work the finest for your body.

The Benefits of Using a Bath Bomb-- Is It Worth It?

When you talk about the advantages of bath bombs, it is essential to focus on the

one significant element that adds to their efficacy. The benefits that you get are hugely based on the kind of essential oils that you use in the bath bomb.

A bath bomb that has the main active ingredient of tea tree oil is a fantastic option to tackle your skincare issues. The application is ideal, too, considering that soaking in the tub will assist you hydrate your skin with the oil.

Another preferred type of essential oil is lavender oil. One of the uses of lavender oil for aromatherapy is for tension reduction. There is nothing as calming as slipping into a warm bath with the aroma of lavender in the air; the enjoyable aroma is wonderfully uplifting. It is a terrific state of mind enhancer.

Essential oils are essential because of the total benefits that bath bombs offer. Each one of these oils has a particular interest. People should experiment with essential oils that provide comparable advantages to discover whether one has more of an impact on you than the others.

Part of this process is to discover the ones that work best for you. This is another reason that a lot of people pick to make their bath bombs, because they may be searching for a specific mix of oils that offers the most significant advantages to them. So embrace your inner scientist and take time to experiment. You will be exceptionally pleased with your results.

What Makes Bath Bombs So Special and remarkable?

Bath bombs have blown up in popularity just recently. Each year the demand for them seems to be increasing as customers discover how amazing bath bombs genuinely are. The market has had a hard time to keep up with this increasing demand.

There are still lots of out there who are uninformed of the incredible benefits of bath bombs. Much of these very same people are searching for 100% natural methods to take on health issues and don't realize that bath bombs are a simple way to bring a healthy and spa-like home.

Recover and Nourish Your Skin.

Among the first remarks you get with routine users of bath bombs is how remarkable it makes their skin look and feel, how it is smoother, and more resistant to blemishes. A few of this can be credited to one of the primary ingredients: baking soda. The fantastic aspect of baking powder is that it has the propensity to soften the bathwater, which makes it more nourishing, gentle, and less abrasive to your skin.

Depending upon your location, your bath water can see a variety of chemical treatments. This chemical residue can hide in your water and can have negative results on your skin. Sodium bicarbonate is an ideal method to combat this concern, offering a simple, proven, and low-cost option.

Another problem is that warm water tends to drain pipes wetness from your skin, which can leave you with the feared alligator skin, both extremely dry and flaky to the touch. Essential oils that moisturize your skin is a great way to deal with this issue. The correct essential oils can keep your skin moisturized and soft, even in the most popular water. Two of my outright favorite crucial oils for skincare are lavender and tea tree. Both work remarkably well, along with having an enjoyable fragrance. Other essential oils help nourish the skin, so do not hesitate to experiment to discover the right one for you.

The Exhilarating Scent of Freshness.

All of us wish to feel very clean and fresh after we bathe. Smelling incredible, too, is a fantastic benefit, naturally. If you put your nose approximately a bath bomb, the very first thing that will likely strike you is the pungent fragrance radiating off of it. We all have different tastes, but it should not be too tough to discover a bath bomb that smells amazing to you.

The factor you wish to take notice of this fragrance is that when the baking powder and citric acid trigger in the water, this is the aroma that will waft through your restroom. These scents also have a method of staying with you for days as they have worked themselves deep into your skin.

Be aware that periodically some people are not fond of the way the fragrance smells on them; our body chemistries are all different and respond differently. You can always test this by watering down a few drops of the active essential oil in a provider oil like coconut or olive oil and dab it on your skin. You can then tell how the scent will react to your body chemistry.

Some people will attempt to layer aromas upon each other. They will start with a bath bomb and then utilize a body lotion as a matching fragrance.

Bath bombs are fantastic for helping individuals clean and unwind away from the stress of the day. Not just can they make you feel fresh physically, but they can influence your mindset, too.

Playing in the Bath is Fun

Let's face it. We all take pleasure in having a little fun with our bath time and bath bombs. No matter what your age, it is difficult not to be entranced by these carbonated little delights. When bath bombs splash into the water, they can fizz, dissolve, and foam, launching a remarkable selection of vivid colors. It resembles a firework goes off in the bath, and depending upon the size of the bath bomb; it can be rather substantial. A few of them have the extra benefit of coloring the water, which is thrilling to experience.

Does it sound like something children would enjoy? You have some issues over the active ingredients. Don't worry; there are bath bombs explicitly made for kids that do not contain any acidic active ingredients. Instead, these bombs are made with soap so that they can be no unintentional harm to your kids or their more delicate skin. Don't expect them to moisturize their skin, however. They are mostly something fun for your kids throughout bath time.

Now, all of these advantages of bath bombs should be sounding amazing, but it is suggested that when you first begin, purchasing your bath bombs might be a fantastic way to experiment. When you have a much better idea of the benefits and scents you are looking for, you can try making your own.

CHAPTER TEN

Usage Of Bath Bomb

How to Use Bath Bombs in Bath

For using bath bombs in the bath, you just need to unwrap the weapons and drop them in your bathroom. After cutting, do not get into the tub instantly. Instead, wait patiently and allow the bombs to fizz and release the moisturizing and aromatic essential oils into the water.

When the oils and other nutritious ingredients get wholly soaked up into the water, step into it to relax and relieve your body and mind. Get a kick out of its mind-blowing scent while cleaning your body with the aromatic nutrient-rich water.

How to Use Bath Bombs in Shower

To use bath bombs in the shower, you have to take out their cover and put them on the floor of the shower. Release the rain in its full circulation and await a while.

The nutritive bombs will start discharging their aromatic and advantageous natural active ingredients into the flowing stream of water. Stand under the open shower to refresh and relax your mind and body with the fragrant water. If you wish to take the best advantage of fragrant bath bombs in the shower, consistently place them in the direct flow of the rain.

How Should Many Bath Bombs be Used?

Bath bombs being fragranced with essential and fragrant oils enhance the satisfaction and enjoyment of having a shower or bath. These bombs are available in various sizes, colors, and shapes, and you can easily pick them according to your requirement. The big bath bombs fizz in the bath for around 5 to 10 minutes making the entire restroom fragrant. As such, one weapon suffices to take a shower for a single time. Interestingly, you can keep the majority of the bath bombs after having a bath and can use it again for many bathes in the future.

CHAPTER ELEVEN

Creating The Right Care and PackagingFor Your Bath Bombs

Whether you are choosing to make your bath bombs and save them in the house for when you need them most, or you are thinking of making bath bombs for offering as a side home service, you need to make sure that the bath bombs are safely kept. Because you are utilizing salt, baking soda, and some essential oils, they are not always going to be the sturdiest, and if you are keeping these incorrectly, all of it can fall apart and make a mess. If you are offering these to other clients, it most likely isn't an excellent concept to send these out and have them arrive as a massive mess on the floor when the consumer opens it up.

Fortunately is that you will be able to evacuate the bath bombs so that they are going to be as safe as possible along the way. This chapter is going to reveal to you some of the techniques that you can use to properly save and package your bath bombs to guarantee that they are going to remain as safe as possible for the long term.

Saving Your Bath Bomb

There are some techniques that you can use to keep your bath bomb properly. Some of the methods that you can use are:

Wrap it

Among the best approaches that you can utilize to take care of your bath bombs is to cover them up. You can use a stick film to wrap them up, and after that keep up on a rack, so they run out the method. If you intend to transfer them to somewhere else, some bubble wrap is going to help you out. Even when you are wrapping the bath bombs, you are dealing with something quite delicate and will have the possibility to crumble easily. Also, when they are finished up, treat them carefully, and only touch them as much as you need before putting them away.

Box it

The most elegant way for you to hold onto the bath bombs and make sure that you are able to utilize them, later on, is to put them inside of boxes. Pick out a bigger box so that you can position more of the bath bombs within, however, make sure that they are put in reasonably tight so that you don't have to stress about them moving around and breaking in the process.

Hang them up

Think about discovering a little wall mount that you can put someplace on the wall in your restroom. You can then put all of the bath bombs inside of this, and then whenever you are prepared to take a bath with one of these, and you can just take them out and are great to go. Make sure that you put it somewhere that is going to be safe and won't get any of the unused bath bombs all breaking and damp apart.

The things to ConsiderBath Bombs

No matter where you are choosing to place the bath bombs, make sure that you are keeping them as far from any form of wetness as possible. When some water hits the weapons, they are going to begin collapsing up since that is what they are designed to do. This is why it isn't usually advised to leave these visible or perhaps in the bathroom because the moisture that originates from there can make it a discomfort to deal with keeping the bath bombs undamaged and ready to utilize.

It is best to wrap these bath bombs up as much as possible. Put them in a space that is not going to get as much moisture, so keep away from the bathroom; and if you reside in an area that gets damp, you ought to consider finding a dryer location or utilizing a dehumidifier to keep the wetness far from the bombs until you are all set to use them. Including in some silica gel pouches is a terrific way to get some of the moisture while also making sure that the bath bombs stay safe and sound.

Heat is also going to be a problem when you are dealing with these bath bombs. The temperature around you can negatively impact the bath bombs, so make sure that they are as far from your heat source as you can get and place in a container that is not going to bring in the heat.

Lights can sometimes cause a bit of staining to the bath bombs if you are not mindful. It is necessary to choose a dark and dry location to leave these bath bombs. Any type of light source, whether you are handling natural light or the light source in the space, can make it challenging to keep the bath bombs in the best working order. Choosing a dark box or inside of a pantry can be the very best way to keep the bath bombs away from the light sources that can make it not exercise well.

There are also a couple of chemicals that will not respond well with the bath bombs, and you will need to ensure that your bath bombs are kept away from them. These chemicals are typically severe, and they are going to trigger some damage to the bath bombs. Things like floor cleaners and phenols are going to move their smells over to the weapon, which can make it less productive and can even cause some concerns on your skin. It is best to choose a safe place to keep these bath bombs far from any of the chemicals that can get into the bath bomb and make them less effective.

And finally, you require to make sure that you are keeping away the bath bomb from plastics. Often some of the chemicals that are inside the plastic products, causing them not to work out that well. This is why it is best to store the bath bombs in a glass or wood container to make sure that it remains neutral. If you do require to utilize a container that is made of plastic, ensure that you wrap it up with some stick movie before you place them inside the box, to make sure that you are keeping the bath bomb safe and effective.

These are some of the crucial things that you can keep track of when you are making your bath bombs. Making sure that you package up the bath bombs adequately and guaranteeing that you are picking the right location to store your bath bomb so that they don't get destroyed can make a massive distinction in how you can look after how the bath bomb will work.

CHAPTER TWELVE

Some Common Mistakes To Be AvoidedIn Making Bath Bombs

When you are first getting started with dealing with bath bombs, you will find that it can be a bit tough. Bath bombs are a great invention and can help you out with a lot of different disorders, and so on, but they are often a bit tough to make, and when you are not used to utilizing them, you will discover that it is simple to make some mistakes. This chapter is going to spend a long time looking at the common mistakes that take place when you are starting with bath bombs and a few of the methods that you will be able to avoid these mistakes when you are working on your very first bath bomb.

Falling apart

The first concern that you might observe when you are working on bath bombs is crumbling or other cracking in the bath bombs. You are going to see that the bath bomb is going to be quite fragile, and it is quite natural for them to fall apart and break. Because it is not going to be able to stick together as well as you would hope, this is typically going to occur when the bath bomb is a bit too dry.

The method that you are going to be able to do this is to ensure to use a bit more of the essential oils that you are taking into the bath bomb, to guarantee that you will have the ability to keep everything entirely. You should also ensure that you aren't packing in the bath bombs too much, or they will crumble together excessive. Adding a bit of vegetable oil to your hands while dealing with the bath bomb can also exercise well because it will help you to get an excellent grasp on the bomb while you are dealing with it, and makes sure that you will get it to all packed in perfectly without the falling apart.

Softening

It's essential to make sure that you aren't adding excessive wetness to the bath bomb, or you are going to wind up with one that is way too soft and won't hold together. This is why the determining part of the formula is so essential because you desire to make sure that you get enough of the moisture to keep the bath bomb together, however not a lot that you are going to have the bath bomb breaking down since it is too soft. It might be an excellent concept to utilize some measuring spoons and jars to make confident that you are getting in the correct amount each time.

The technique for getting the correct amount of moisture into everyone is going to depend on the components that you are using inside the bath bomb. If you discover that you are putting in too much wetness and the mix is getting too soft, ensure to add in a bit of starch to the mixture to make it a bit firmer. Be cautious about including in water to the bath bomb since this can cause a mess with the item.

Swellings

There are numerous factors that you might end up with some swellings or other bumps inside of your bath bomb. If the baking soda has some of the lumps inside of it, it is going to be hard to make a bath bomb that doesn't have these very same lumps inside of them.

Because of the ingredients that you are using with the oil, another reason that you may have some concerns with clumping is. You will find that some components are not going to work that well with each other, or if you use excessive of one ingredient compared to the other elements, you are going to wind up with some lumps. It is best to generate some determining cups to make sure that all of the ingredients exist inside the bath bomb in the correct amounts each time.

No fizz

When you drop the bath bomb into your bath, you must hear a good fizz sound going off. You will require to make sure to add in a bit more of the citric acid inside to make sure that the bath bomb is going to begin to fizz.

So how do you know that you have enough of the citric acid within your bath bomb? This is going to depend upon the amount of citric acid that is requested at the start of the recipe. These are performed in set quantities, so if you start to add in more of other ingredients, make sure that you are keeping it even with the citric acid as well.

Growth

If you see the bath bomb and it is expanding or not staying inside the mold effectively, it means that you have too much moisture inside either the atmosphere or with the bath bomb. The humidity is going to cause a chemical response that will allow the bomb to expand. You require to make sure that the wetness within the bath bomb or in the air around the bomb is not too much. When the bomb is done being made, you ought to ensure that you cover it up expertly and keep some of the wetness to make sure that you are keeping it safe without including in some more moisture.

Discoloration

When the bath bomb is in the air, there is, in some cases, going to be concerns with discoloration. This is primarily since the air particles are going to react in a particular way with the bomb, and this can cause it to lose the color. This is going to vary based upon the active ingredients that remain in the bath bomb, but it is not going to impact how the bath bomb is going to perform. Make sure that you include in some more food coloring to keep it going well if you would like to make sure that the bomb keeps the best color.

Shapeless bomb

There are extended times when it is going to be hard for you to keep the shape that you want with your bath bomb. This is often going to take place if the weapon is too moist or too dry. This is going to trigger the bath bomb to not fit into the mold, and it is hard to get it to form into any shape at all. The very best option is to see how the wetness is carrying out in the bath bomb and make the best changes.

These are some of the most common bath bombs that you will be able to delight in when you are very first starting on this job in your own house. You may discover that for the very first few batches of these you make, it is going to be a bit tough, and you may see that this is going to be something that you will need to deal with in the beginning. After some practice and finding out what works, the best for your needs while making these bath bombs, you will have the ability to develop the item that works the finest for you.

CHAPTER THIRTEEN

Natural Bath Bomb Recipes To Help You Get Started

When you are ready to get begun with some bath bombs, make sure to have a look at these simple alternatives that will help to provide you the best bath ever, while also making sure that you get something that smells and feels fantastic!

Peppermint and Chocolate Bath Bomb

Ingredients:

- 4 tsp. peppermint oil
- 4 oz. coconut oil
- 1 c. honey powder
- 4 oz. vegetable glycerin
- 12 Tbsp. cocoa powder
- 4 oz. cocoa butter
- 1 c. buttermilk powder
- 2 c. citric acid
- 4 c. baking powder
- 3 c. cornstarch
- 12 Tbsp. parsley powder.
- 2 c. Epsom salt

Directions:

1. To get going with this recipe, take out a double broiler and include the cocoa butter. Let this melt gradually. Include in the veggie glycerin and coconut oil and blend well once this is melted. Remove the broiler and set aside.

2. As this rests, get a huge bowl and add in the baking soda and Epsom salt and use your hand to blend them until all the swellings are gone. Include in the peppermint essential oil and mix well.

3. Now take the cornstarch, honey powder, buttermilk powder, and citric acid and blend them in with the Epsom salt mix. Divide this mixture in between two bowls.

4. Include the cocoa powder to one bowl and the parsley powder to the other and mix well.

5. Put half of your butter mix into the dishes. Knead it thoroughly and then scoop a little the mixture from the bowl. Mold this into a small bomb, and after that, repeat till the mixture is gone.

6. Include the remainder of the butter mix to the 2nd bowl. Scoop a bit out of the bowl and form into bath bombs. Put these onto a flat pan and let them rest for 24 hours or two to make them solidify.

7. Serve these in an excellent container. When you are prepared to use, pop a few of these into the bathwater and take pleasure in.

Heart Bombs

Ingredients:

- 12 Tbsp. grapefruit essential oil
- Witch hazel spray 4 Tbsp.
- Pink Brazilian Clay 2 Tbsp.
- Jojoba oil 2 c.
- Citric acid1 c.
- Epsom salt4 c.
- Baking soda Heart molds

Directions:

1. Take out a big bowl and add in the Epsom salt, citric acid, and baking soda inside. Mix them all well.

2. When this is ready, include in the grapefruit essential oil and blend it well. Include in the jojoba oil and mix up until it is a great powder.

3. Leave the first bowl alone, but include in the pink Brazilian clay to the stuff that remains in the second bowl and mix well. Use the witch hazel to spray over both dishes and knead them both well so that it starts to stick together. Include in a little jojoba oil and knead some more.

4. Transfer this mix over to the heart-shaped molds and then let them rest for 24 hours so that they end up being hard when this is done, relocation over to an airtight container.

5. When you are prepared to utilize, pop a couple of into the tub and, after that, fill it with warm water before taking pleasure in.

Eucalyptus Bomb

Ingredients:

- 20 tsp. eucalyptus oil

- Silicone molds

- 10 drops food coloring, green

- 2 tsp. Water

- 5 tsp. grapeseed oil

- 30 drops lime oil

- 1/2 c. cream of tartar

- 2 c. baking soda

- 1 c. cornstarch

1 c. Epsom salts

Instructions:

1. Draw out a huge bowl and include in the Epsom salt, cream of tartar, cornstarch, and baking soda and blend them all correctly.

2. In a bowl, gather the grapeseed oil before including the eucalyptus oil, water, lime oil, and food coloring. Mix these around thoroughly for the oils to mix.

3. Now you can pour the oil mixture into the bowl with the baking soda and after that utilize the mixer to get all the ingredients to blend well.

4. When the mix is complimentary of lumps, transfer to a silicone mold and press it in vigorously. Allow this to rest for

about 24 hours and let them get solid. Store in an airtight container.

Lemon Bomb

Ingredients:

- Molds
- 60 drops yellow food coloring
- Water
- 40 drops lemon oil
- 1 c. Epsom salt
- 4 c. citric acid
- 4 c. baking soda
- 4 c. cornstarch

Instructions:

1. To get started with this recipe, get a big bowl and combine the Epsom salt, citric acid, cornstarch, and baking soda and guarantee that they are all blended well.

2. Pour the lemon oil into this bowl and mix once again before adding in the yellow food coloring. Add in a bit of water as a spray to assist the active ingredients in binding together well.

3. Move this mix over to a mold and utilize your fingers to push this into the patterns firmly. Let these set to the side for about 24 hours or more to

make the mixture excellent and challenging.

4. Shop until you are ready to utilize in a nice warm bath.

Orange Bombs

Ingredients:

- Orange food coloring 4 Tbsp. water
- 2 tsp. Orange oil 1 c. Epsom salt
- 2 c. citric acid
- 4 c. baking soda
- 2 c. cornstarch

Instructions:

1. Bring out a big bowl and add in the Epsom salt, citric acid, cornstarch, and baking soda, putting in the time to make sure they mix well. Gather the orange oil and blend well again.

2. Now you can add in the orange food coloring, including as much as you would like to get the ideal color of orange.

3. Take a bit of the water and simply mist it over the mix. This water will be used to assist you in binding the components together well.

4. Transfer this mixture over to the molds and push them in firmly. Let the shapes set for at least 24 hours so that it has time to harden and will leave the pattern quickly.

5. Store these into an airtight container and after that place into some warm water in your next bath.

Lavender Bombs

Ingredients:

- Purple food coloring 8 tsp.
- Epsom salt 32 oz.

Instructions

1. Get a big bowl and include the Epsom salt, cream of tartar, cornstarch, and baking soda inside. Make sure that they are mixed well.

2. Get another bowl and gather the coconut oil. Add in the lavender oil,

filtered water, and food coloring. If required, blend them well and include in a few more drops of lavender oil.

3. Put this oil into the bowl with baking soda, going slowly. Utilize a mixer to finish mixing them.

4. Move the mixture over to a silicone mold and use your fingers to push these within firmly. Allow the shells to set for a minimum of 24 hours so that they have time to solidify.

5. Pour a little out of these into your bath water when you are ready and enjoy!

Peppermint and Eucalyptus Bath Bomb Ingredients:

- 1 c. Epsom salt
- 2 c. cornstarch
- 1 c. water
- 2 c. citric acid
- 20 drops eucalyptus oil 4 c. baking soda
- 20 drops peppermint Directions:

Instructions

1. To start this recipe, bring out a bowl and then place the Epsom salt, citric acid, cornstarch, and baking soda together, making sure that they are blended well.

2. Inside another bowl, include in the eucalyptus oil. Include in the peppermint oil and the water to this and mix the oils well.

3. Now you can pour the oils into the bowl with the sodium bicarbonate, going gradually. Use a mixer to blend these up until they are equally mixed, ensuring that there aren't any lumps inside.

4. Press this mix into the mold, making sure that it is securely pushed in

and then set to the side so that these can end up being firm over the next 24 hours.

5. Shop these in a safe place until you are prepared to use it in a warm bath.

Bergamot and Lavender Bombs

Ingredients:

- 1 c. Epsom salt
- 2 c. cornstarch
- 1 c. water
- 2 c. citric acid
- 20 drops bergamot oil 1 c. baking soda
- 20 drops lavender oil Directions:

Instructions

1. Inside a big bowl, include the Epsom salt, citric acid, cornstarch, and baking soda, making sure that they are blended well.

2. Inside another blending bowl, gather the lavender oil inside. Include the bergamot and the water-oil as well and mix till the oils are well combined.

3. Put the oil mixture into the bowl with the sodium bicarbonate, mixing as you go. Make sure that the ingredients are all combined well up until there are no swellings.

4. Take this mix and press it into the molds of your choice, pressing down actively to get it all packed in.

5. Set these to the side and let them rest for at least 24 hours until they are firm enough. Store in a dry and cool location and then use the bath bomb in warm water when you are ready.

Tea Tree and Mint Bath Bombs Ingredients:

- 1 c. Epsom salt
- 2 c. cornstarch
- 2 c. citric acid
- 10 drops mint oil 1 c. water
- 10 drops tea tree oil 4 c. baking soda
- 20 drops sage oil

Directions:

1. To start this recipe, draw out a big bowl and integrate the Epsom salt, citric acid, cornstarch, and baking soda. Ensure that these are all blended well.

2. Get a blending bowl and gather the tea tree oil and the sage oil. Make sure that they are well integrated before adding the mint oil and the water and then blending around a bit more.

3. When the oils are well mixed, pour them in with the baking soda mixture, and after that, draw out your hand mixer to blend them all to make even and eliminate the swellings.

4. Get your silicone molds and utilize your fingers to press the mixture inside the shapes firmly. Pack them securely and set the ways to the side to solidify over the next 24 hours.

5. Store them properly and then toss a few into a warm water bath the next time that you need them as soon as these are dry.

Rose Oil and Lavender Bath Bombs

Ingredients:

- 2 c. cornstarch
- Ten drops rose oil 2 c. citric acid
- 4 c. baking soda
- 10 drops geranium oil 1 c. Epsom salt
- 1 c. water
- 20 drops lavender oil

Instructions

1. Take out a bowl and the Epsom salt, citric acid, cornstarch, and baking soda. Ensure that they are well combined.

2. Take out another bowl and include the geranium oil and the lavender oil and blend gently.

3. Add the rose oil and the water in with the other two oils and blend everything together until smooth. When these are all set, put them in with the baking soda and mix, either by hand or with a hand mixer till they are soft and the swellings are gone.

4. When this mixture is combined, use your fingers to push it into the molds firmly. Set these molds to the side and let them solidify for the next 24 hours.

5. When these are solidified, keep them properly and then use them in a warm bath whenever you need them.

Cedarwood and Orange Bath Bomb

Ingredients:

- 1 c. cornstarch
- 5 drops orange oil 1/2 c. water
- 1 c. citric acid
- Five drops lemon oil 5 drops clove oil 2 c. baking soda
- 1/2 c. Epsom salt
- 5 drops cedarwood oil

Instructions

1. Get a bowl and then include the Epsom salt, citric acid, cornstarch, and baking soda, making sure that they are well combined.

2. Bring out another bowl and mix in the clove oil and the cedarwood oil together, blending well before including in the lemon oil.

3. Now, add in the orange oil and the water to the other oils and mix them well. Put this into the bowl with the sodium bicarbonate, going slowly, and utilize a mixer to combine them all and to eliminate the swellings.

4. With the use of your fingers, press this mix into a mold of your choice, making sure that it gets in there tight. Set these molds aside and let them solidify for a minimum of 24 hours.

5. After these have had time to solidify, put them into an airtight container, and then use them inside a warm bath when you are set or ready.

Lavender and Sage Bath Bomb

Ingredients:

- Witch hazel spray ten drops
- castor oil 3/4 oz
- lavender flower powder ten drops
- Bentonite clay 32 oz.
- green soap colorant
- olive oil 60 drops
- Forty drops of sage oil 1 1/8 oz
- citric acid 60 oz.
- baking soda
- 40 drops of lavender oil

Directions

1. To begin this recipe, draw out a big bowl and integrate the lavender flower powder, citric acid, bentonite clay, and baking soda. Ensure that they are combined well.

2. Get another bowl and pour in the lavender oil and the essential oil, blending well before including in the green soap colorant.

3. Now add the olive oil and the castor oil to the rest of the oils and blend well. Pour this mixture into the bowl with the sodium bicarbonate and use a mixer to mix them entirely in a flat style, inspecting to see if the components are mixed well.

4. Take the mixture and pack it in with your fingers to the silicone molds.

Enable these to rest for a minimum of 24 hours and let them get hard.

5. When the mix is hardened, you can take them out of the molds, place them in an airtight storage container, and then use it in a warm bath whenever you would like.

Aloe Bubble Bath Bomb

Ingredients:

- 2 c. citric acid
- 1/4 c. Basmati rice oil Witch hazel
- Irish green colorant 1/2 oz.
- Kentish rain fragrance- 8
- leaf wax tart molds
- 4 c. baking soda
- 2 c. salt
- Lauryl sulfate acetate
- 20 oz. aloe extract

Directions:

1. For this recipe, you can get a big bowl and add the citric acid and baking soda. Now include the sodium mix to the sodium bicarbonate and use your hands to get them all to blend.

2. Draw out the colorant that you are using and add it to the mixture, going one drop at a time up until you end up with the color that you would like. Now included in the aloe extract, rain fragrance oil, and the basmati rice oil.

3. If the mix is a bit dry for you, you can include a little the witch hazel spray to help them bind together well. Ensure that it is devoid of lumps too.

4. When you are done with this, bring out the molds and use your fingers to pack the mix inside firmly. Permit these to rest for a minimum of 24 hours so that they have time to harden.

5. When you are ready to use, pop a few of these into your bath water and delight in the terrific bath!

Oatmeal Bath Bomb

Ingredients:

- 12 tsp. almond oil 10 drops food coloring of choice 1/2 c. oatmeal
- 4 Tbsp. water
- 1 c. citric acid
- 30 drops lemon oil
- 2 1/2 c. baking soda

Directions:

1. Draw out a bowl and add in the citric acid, oatmeal, and baking soda, making sure that they are well blended. Add the food coloring to this bowl as well.

2. Now bring out another bowl and gather the lemon oil and the almond oil.

Mix them well to make sure that the oils mix well.

3. Pour this oil mix into a huge bowl with the baking soda and then utilize a mixer to mix them thoroughly.

4. Take a little bit of water and spray it around the mix a bit so that it can assist the components in binding together a bit better.

5. Once the combination is all out of swellings, you can draw out your molds and then make use of your fingers to press the mixture into the molds. Set these to the side and let it harden for the next 24 hours.

6. After this time, store the bath bomb appropriately, then pop them into the warm water of your bath whenever you require.

Blueberry Bath Bombs

Ingredients:

- Witch hazel - 3/4 oz.
- Fruit powder - 1 1/8 oz.
- blue colorant
- 60 drops blueberry fragrance oil
- 64 oz. citric acid
- 50 oz. baking soda
- 2 1/2 oz. Sweet Almond oil

Directions:

1. To start this recipe, draw out a bowl and include in the citric acid and baking soda. When this is combined well, add the fruit powder and mix.

2. Take out the colorant and slowly add it to the mix, doing one drop at a time. Enjoy the mix and stop including the dye when you have the color of blue that you would like.

3. When you have the right blue inside, include the blueberry oil and almond oil and mix everything in together. Spray a little bit of the witch hazel over the mix to assist the components in binding together well.

4. When the active ingredients are without lumps, use your fingers to press this into the silicone molds of your option. Set

these to the side and let them harden for a minimum of 24 hours.

5. After the time is up, take the bombs out of the molds and save them properly until you are all set to utilize in a warm bat

CHAPTER FOURTEEN

The Fundamentals of Goat Milk Soap

When you choose to make 100 percent goat milk soap, any kind of recipe you have will do. You'll simply replace goat milk for the water required in the method. Past that, making soap with goat milk is a bit different from making soap with water-- nonetheless, it's so worth the extra problem!

Not every person will have the luxury of having fresh goat milk, so if this holds with you, you'll need to make use of either canned or powdered milk.

If it isn't put in a fridge or freezer, goat milk soap will certainly turn wheat-colored. The hotter it becomes, the darker it will undoubtedly go. If you like your soap to be white, put it in the fridge as rapidly as you put it in the mold.

Soap made with canned and powdered milk will certainly not be as white as soap made with fresh juice.

Making Goat Milk Soap

Similar to other types of soap, you need to assemble the tools you'll require beforehand. After you start, you will certainly not have time to look for something! Below's what you'll need:

- Safety glasses
- Thin latex gloves
- Scale
- Plastic pitcher
- Cereal dish-- dimension glass or plastic bowls (for oils and butters).
- Long-handled stainless-steel or plastic spoon.
- Meat or pleasant thermometer.
- Immersion blender or food processor.
- Freezer paper.
- Mold
- Stove.

One Hundred Percent Goat Milk Soap

When the milk fumes, the sugars in it transform dark, making the soap brown. That's similarly why the soap goes via gel in the refrigerator.

Here's what is required:

Weight of Oils - 11 ounces.

Water as % of Oils - 34

Super Fat % - 10

Fragrance Oz per Pound - 7.

Goat milk - 77.691 grams (2.74 ounces).

Lye-- salt hydroxide - 40.023 grams (1.412 ounces).

Palm oil - 187.107 grams (6.6 ounces) (60%).

Castor oil - 62.369 grams (2.2 ounces) (20%).

Coconut oil - 31.184 grams (1.1 ounces) (10%).

Sunflower (High Oleic) 31.184 grams (1.1 ounces) (10%).

Right here are the soap qualities:

Hardness - 39

Cleansing - 7

Conditioning - 59

Bubbly - 25

Creamy - 49

Iodine - 58

INS - 142

Freeze the goat milk before you start making this soap. Do this with whichever type you make use of-- tinned, powdered, or fresh. If you want it frozen solid pour about 77.691 grams (2.74 ounces) of goat milk into a zipper-lock bag, as well as lay it level in the fridge freezer. Before you include it to the recipe, go down the packet on the counter or the floor a couple of times to dissolve the frozen milk right into pieces. (This works better than striking it with a hammer, which may damage the bag and cause a big mess.) Regularly wear your gloves and unbreakable glass before you start.

Directions

1. Line your mold with freezer paper (glossy side up). If you're making use of a plastic tray mold and mildew, you do not need to line it, however, using a cooking or silicone mold spray will assist the soap launch from the frame more comfortable.

2. Weigh the fragrance oil and established it aside.

3. Consider the lye, and also set it aside. Make sure it has a cover on it so it won't spill.

4. Establish the pot over reduced warm, as well as heat till all the oils are thawed.

5. When the oils get to 95 ° F, get rid of the milk from the freezer, and also drop it on the counter to damage into items.

6. Put the lye over the frozen items of milk, and even stir slowly until all the liquid and lye are liquified. Do not hurry this action; every one of the lye and also milk must liquify.

7. When the lye/milk are liquified, gradually include them to the cooled oil mix, and mix with a spoon.

8. Include the fragrance oil and stir to integrate. The cucumber mint does not accelerate the soap to trace, so you can use the immersion blender if you wish.

9. As soon as the soap starts to enlarge, put it right into the all set mold. Due to the truth that of the high sugar in the milk, the soap will transform dark if you enable it to go into gel mode.

10. If you do not prefer your soap to dim, place it in the refrigerator as quickly as you put it right into the mold. Thirty-six hours is better because it's much less probably to be lye-active after that long, and also, the added air conditioning time takes a few of the moisture out of the soap.

11. Take the soap out from the mold, cut into bars, and permit to dry completely. You might have lye activity up to 48 hours after putting into the mold and mildew.

12. Because of the reality that this soap has 20 percent castor oil, it requires to treat for 4 to 6 weeks before using. The soap won't injure you if you use it right currently; it just won't be as moisturizing. It merely takes the consisted of time for the lye to make the castor oil let go of its marvel- ful moisturizing top qualities. It's well worth the wait.

Fifty Percent Goat Milk/50 Percent Water Soap.

Considering that you do not have to freeze the milk initially, this recipe is a bit much easier as well as much less lengthy than the 100 Percent Goat Milk Soap recipe earlier in this phase. This recipe can yield about 15.7 ounces (445.1 grams) of soap.

Here's what you would require:

- Weight of Oils - 11 ounces.
- Water as % of Oils - 38.
- Super Fat % - 8.
- Fragrance Oz per Pound - 7 PPO.
- Distilled water - 38.840 grams (1.37 ounces)
- Lye
- Salt hydroxide - 40.023 grams (1.41 ounces)
- Goat milk - 38.840 grams (1.37 ounces).
- Hand oil - 6.6 ounces (187.107 grams) (60%) Coconut oil - 1.1 ounces (31.184 grams) (10%) Castor oil - 2.2 ounces (62.369 grams) (20%) Sunflower (high oleic) - 1.1 ounces (31.184 grams) (10%)
- Cucumber-mint fragrance oil - 48 ounce (13.640 grams) (.7 ppo).

Here are the soap qualities:.

Hardness - 39.

Cleansing - 7

Conditioning - 59

Bubbly - 25

Velvety - 49.

Iodine - 58

INS- 142.

Make sure you always wear your gloves and shatterproof glass before you start.

Directions

1. Line the base of your mold with freezer paper (shiny side up), adhering to the guidelines earlier stated. You don't have to line it if you are making use of a plastic tray mold.

2. Evaluate the fragrance oil, as stated.

3. Evaluate the water, and add the lye. Stir till dissolved.

4. Consider the milk, and also established it apart in its container.

5. Consider each oil as well as consist of to the pot. If you get the oils too warm, allow them to cool down to the ideal temperature level.

6. When the oils have cooled to about 95 ° F, collect the fragrance oils, and also mix with the immersion mixer. Or you may wait until the soap traces properly to include the fragrance, if you like.

7. Add the milk to the lye/water blend, stir, as well as right now take into the oils. Do not allow the lye/water/milk to establish for any kind of time, or it will certainly start to turn orange an also smell. As quickly as you consist of the liquid to the lye/water combination, include it to the oils.

8. Change to a spatula or spoon, so you can feel the soap as it gets thicker. The immersion mixer brings the soap to the map quicker, and also the fragrance oil accelerates it, too. The soap will zoom right on previous light trace as well as be as well keen to put directly into the mold.

9. Place the soap right into the lined mold, as well as place directly into the refrigerator for 24 to 36 hrs.

10. Take out the soap from the mold and mildew, cut into bars, and also allow to dry completely. Let at the very least about four weeks pass before you make use of the soap. It will be a lot more moisturizing than when first made if you wait.

Castor oil is one of the hardest oil to saponify, and it will undoubtcdly take about four weeks for the lye to make the castor oil lose its outstanding qualities to the soap.

CONCLUSION

There has been a substantial boost in the number of individuals who are aiming to make their homemade products to be used on their bodies and to keep their house tidy and clear. People are tired of all the chemicals that remain in their store purchased items, and they like the concept that they can control the ingredients of these products when they make them at home while saving a lot of money.

This book has invested some time talking about what bath bombs are and how you will be able to make them at home whenever you want. Make sure to read this guidebook and see what you can do with the assistance of homemade bath bombs!